I AM...

'Look! Taste and see for yourself... There is none like
Christ — none like this one who said, "I am..."'!
(from the foreword by Geoff Thomas)

'Iain Campbell's meditations help us to eat the bread,
see the light, enter the door, follow the shepherd,
experience the resurrection, travel the way and abide
in the vine that Christ is. Take, read and discover that
Christ really is all that you need.'
(Joel R. Beeke)

I AM…

Exploring the 'I am' sayings of John's Gospel

Iain D. Campbell

 BOOKS

EP Books
Faverdale North, Darlington, DL3 0PH, England
e-mail: sales@epbooks.org
web: www.epbooks.org

133 North Hanover Street, Carlisle, PA 17013, USA.
e-mail: usasales@epbooks.org
web: www.epbooks.us

First published 2011

British Library Cataloguing in Publication Data available

ISBN 13 978 085234 774 4   ISBN 0 85234 774 x

Printed and bound in Great Britain by Martins the Printers,
Berwick upon Tweed

CONTENTS

FOREWORD

There is none like Christ — none at all! None other is
God and man, two natures in one person. None other
has the love, grace and heart of Jehovah Jesus. The
sight of him is so breathtaking that we turn aside at an
opportunity that a glimpse of him affords. We cease
looking at the most precious things in the universe to
gaze and gaze at him. We know little of him, miserably
little. It is our duty and privilege to behold him, and it
is the duty and privilege of each of his preachers to
show him to us. 'Sirs,' we plead with them, 'we would
see Jesus.' Let us contemplate Christ, and let his
servants magnify him before us.

So in these studies Dr Iain D. Campbell does this,
making Christ omni-attractive as he sets him out
through our Lord's self-disclosure, in a series of extraordinary claims Jesus made — to be pre-existent,

the only way to God, the food and the vine of heaven, the good shepherd, the resurrection and the life. Those are words of a megalomaniac if they are not the words of the incarnate God. Examine! Look! Taste and see for yourself. Oh, behold him! Behold him in each great claim, one after another. There is none like Christ — none like this one who said, 'I am...'!

Geoff Thomas

INTRODUCTION

Like the other three Gospels, the Gospel of John gives us a record of Jesus' life, death and resurrection. We have four Gospels, which together give us a great deal of information about the Lord, about what he did and why he did it.

But when we read the Gospel of John, it is not long before we realize that John is different; he is very selective in what he writes. There are some things that the other three Gospels tell us which John does not tell us; for example, there are no parables in the Gospel of John, and there is no record of exorcisms — no stories of demons being cast out. These are just two examples of what John omits from his record.

John is also very different in his style and manner of writing. There are little things that are distinctive about him. For example, John always uses the word 'sign' when he is talking about the miracles. When he tells us about Jesus turning water into wine in Cana of Galilee, he says that it was 'the first of his signs' (2:11). It is the same in 6:2, where John says that a large crowd was following Jesus 'because they saw the signs that he was doing on the sick'.

How do you 'do' a 'sign'? John is telling us that the works of Jesus, and particularly the miracles he per-formed, were actually 'signs', pointers towards, and authenticators of, his messiahship. So in 6:26 the Gos-pel relates these signs to faith, as Jesus accuses the people of following him only for earthly food, and not because of the heavenly signs.

John also uses a very interesting double 'Amen' when he writes. In the older translations of the Bible it was translated as 'verily, verily'; in the ESV it is ren-dered 'truly, truly'. There is something John wants to emphasize and underline. The sayings of Jesus are not only true; they command our attention, and they demand that we listen.

Another of the distinctive features of John's Gospel is that he records seven sayings of Jesus that are not to be found in the other three Gospels, the 'I am' sayings of Jesus. In them, Jesus introduces us to himself by means of a phrase translated 'I am', followed by a description of himself. These are:

I am the bread of life.
I am the light of the world.

I am the door.
I am the good shepherd.
I am the resurrection and the life.
I am the way, the truth and the life.
I am the true vine.

The 'I am' phrase is interesting. John could have expressed this with one Greek word, but he in fact uses two. The first is the very emphatic personal pronoun, 'I', and then the verb, 'I am'. Literally it is 'I, I am'. John's usage is striking. His use of it is very distinctive in chapter 8, where Jesus is speaking to the Jewish leaders who claimed that they were the descendants of Abraham. Jesus accuses them of being totally unlike the father they professed to have. If they were the children of Abraham, they would believe on him. Then Jesus makes the remarkable statement in 8:58: 'Before Abraham was, I am.'

This phrase catches us. It seems to fly against grammatical and historical sense. Jesus is not merely saying that he existed prior to Abraham, but that his existence both predates and postdates Abraham. Before Abraham existed, Jesus claims to have existed, and long after Abraham is gone, he continues to exist.

Jesus is claiming a pre-existence for himself. He is saying that he existed in fact long before he existed in the world. None of us can say that, but Jesus can. He existed before he existed in the world, and even before Abraham existed in the world. He is actually saying that he existed before the world itself existed, which is the point at which John begins his Gospel: 'In the beginning was the Word' (1:1). John begins with an affirmation of the eternalness of Jesus, in words reminiscent of the psalmist when he said:

> Before the mountains were brought forth,
>> or ever you had formed the earth and the world,
>
> from everlasting to everlasting you are God
>> (Psalm 90:2).

But more is going on here. By describing himself as the pre-existent 'I am', Jesus is identifying himself with the way in which God revealed himself in the Old Testament. When Moses was confronted with the burning bush in the wilderness and the voice of God spoke to him, commissioning him to confront Pharaoh with the demand to let his people go, Moses asked, 'What is your name?'

God, in that grand moment of self-disclosure and self-revelation, declares: 'I AM who I AM' (Exodus 3:14). God continues: 'Say this to the people of Israel: "I AM has sent me to you."' Here is the God of the Bible: he is the eternal, unchangeable, glorious God whose name is I AM. And now Jesus applies that designation to himself.

So in the context of the grand Christ of John's Gospel, John picks up these seven distinct sayings of Jesus, all of which expand on the name of Jehovah, the name I AM, the name that belongs to Jesus because he is the God of the Old Testament. The descriptions are linked to the designation 'I AM', and the designation belongs properly to Jehovah.

The seven sayings, then, are rooted and grounded in this revelation, and go on to employ a metaphor, or figurative language, to answer the question: 'Who are you, Jesus?' He is the great I AM who exists from eternity to eternity, and yet comes into our world and says, 'I am the bread of life, the light of the world, the true vine', and so on. These seven sayings are full and deep and rich with meaning and significance. Let's study them together.

1.

JESUS THE BREAD

I am the bread of life

John 6:35

The first of the 'I am' sayings in John's Gospel is: 'I am the bread of life.' It occurs several times in John 6. In verse 41 Jesus says, 'I am the bread that came down from heaven.' In verse 48 he says, 'I am the bread of life'; in verse 51, 'I am the living bread that came down from heaven.' Then, in a different form, in verse 58 he says, 'This is the bread that came down from heaven.' Jesus describes himself in a very simple way, using a picture from everyday life. The great I AM is the bread of life.

In this immediate context Jesus had fed five thousand people with some loaves and some fish. He had won a crowd. There was a large group following him;

even when he withdrew himself, the crowd wanted to know where he was, and they came to him. The following day the crowd that remained wanted Jesus, and when they saw he was not there they got into their boats, crossed the lake and went looking for him.

Then Jesus begins to teach that crowd. He starts to explain to them what he is doing in the world, and what his mission is. He has come; now he is going to teach the crowd the purpose for his coming, and the nature of it.

Ironically, Jesus then loses the crowd. His teaching is offensive; for all its simplicity and naturalness, rooted as it is in earthly life, and filled with easy-to-understand illustrations and analogies, his is an offensive doctrine. Such simple language proves to be too much for hearts and minds hardened by sin. Many of those who followed Jesus at this point walked away and didn't want to walk with him any more.

Isn't it remarkable that the greatest preacher the world has ever heard, who was able to expound the message of God as no one before or after him could, watched as people ignored him and no longer followed him? Like Isaiah, the great Messiah preacher Jesus could say, 'Who has believed our report?' (Isaiah 53:1, NKJV). Jesus is proclaiming the gospel and draws an audience; then he loses it, not because he is a bad teacher, but precisely because he is not. He is a good teacher, who is faithful and deep, who tells the truth as it is. And it is the truth that comes from God that turns the crowd away.

Jesus in this context teaches the crowd by reminding them of the way in which God had fed his people in the wilderness. Bread had literally come to them from heaven to feed the Israelites in the wilderness. For forty years God provided manna for his people in the wilderness. Yet that generation perished. And although there is a similarity between the manna and Jesus, the point is a point of contrast: 'Your fathers ate manna in the wilderness, and Moses in his day spoke about that provision, and they had it, but there is something come now that is even more glorious and lasting: I am the bread of life.'

However glorious that provision in the Old Testament was, it is nothing in comparison with the provision that there is for us now in Jesus Christ. So what is this great statement on the lips of Jesus telling us about what God has provided for us in Christ?

The bread of life is necessary for us

Jesus says that he is the bread of life, and that eating this bread means that you don't go hungry; if you don't eat this bread, you will go hungry. This is the bread that sinners need. Just as bread is the staple diet of our natural life, there is something here that is fundamentally important for our spiritual life, and for our life in the presence of God. Without it we perish and die of hunger, our souls starve and there is nothing to nourish and fill us. If we fill our lives with anything else, it is junk food compared with this food: this is the food that brings life and vitality and health.

It is very interesting to note John's use of the concept of eating in his Gospel. In chapter 4 Jesus had a conversation with a woman, after which someone said to him that no one had given him anything to eat. Do you remember his response? 'I have food to eat that you do not know about... My food is to do the will of him who sent me and to accomplish his work' (4:34).

It is because Jesus ate his 'food' that he is able to meet our needs. He ate the food of obedience to the Father's will, and that is what makes him such a glorious provision for our own souls. We can come to him, and we can 'eat'; indeed, we *must* eat this bread. We are not called to die on the cross as he did; he did all that was necessary for our salvation. It was through eating that we lost communion with God: Adam ate forbidden food and all mankind fell into sin. And it is also by eating the bread of God's providing that life and vitality are restored to our souls. If we do not eat, we die in our sins.

Have we discovered that without Jesus we perish? In the gospel life and death are set before us, blessing and cursing, heaven and hell: these are the issues with which the gospel is concerned, and they affect every individual in the world, whatever their circumstances or age.

Jesus is the difference between living and dying, between being condemned in our sins and having life. He is absolutely necessary. The devil is quite happy if he can convince people that they don't need him, or that they don't need him yet, or that they need him only after everything else has been dealt with. But this is all a lie: Jesus is the one thing needful; whatever we have or do not have, unless this Jesus-bread is in our soul, and unless his work is applied to us personally, we shall die in our sins. By describing himself as the bread of heaven, Jesus is reminding me that I must have him if I am to have life.

The bread of heaven is suitable for us

Whoever I may be, the bread of heaven is suitable for me. Jesus says, 'I am the bread of life; *whoever* eats will live.' Whoever eats — it is suitable for everyone. When it comes to food, we all have different tastes: there are some things we like and dislike. Sometimes what is tasty is bad for us; what is good for us does not always appear very appetizing.

But Jesus is sweet to our taste, and suitable for us all. No one eats this bread and discovers that they are allergic to it, or that they have an intolerance for it. For every boy and girl, every man and woman, this bread is suitable; it is able to meet needs that nothing else can meet. It can give strength where nothing else can give strength, and sustain where nothing else can sustain. There is something here suitable for us all.

Only Jesus can offer himself in a way that meets every need. We are not required to know everything about him, or everything about what it means to follow him. We are not required to understand everything that the Bible says about him. It is enough to know that we are hungry and that bread is provided: all that is necessary is that you realize that you are a sinner and that Jesus is the Saviour.

That means that he meets all our conditions. Every need he can supply. Every blemish he can wipe away. Every sin he can forgive. The bread is his life, given for the world. That is why he is a suitable provision: because of his life given over at Calvary. All the sins we committed can be dealt with. Whether they are old or new, he remains suitable for sinners, beyond change. On the basis of his spotless life and matchless death, on the basis of Calvary's completed transaction, Jesus can legitimately claim that he is the bread of life.

The bread of life is available for us

This bread is there for the taking. It is within the reach of every one of us. Many of us in the Western world do not know what it is to lack for food. We go to our

supermarkets, and the shelves are full. It is not like
that in some countries of the world; there are places
where food is not available, it is so scarce. But here is
bread, and it is available. It is not simply for other
people; Jesus says that it is within our reach. It is
available for all.

There is a marvellous point of comparison with the
manna here. The manna covered the wilderness floor
and God said there was enough for all. Taken on God's
terms, there was enough for everyone. By gathering in
each day, and by taking in two days' worth on the sixth
day, in order to honour the Sabbath, the Israelites
discovered that there was enough there for all.

Everyone and anyone could have it. There is an
unconditional and absolute offer here for sinners to
come. Jesus says that this bread has come *down* from
heaven. How can I know that I am going to heaven?
The gospel comes with the news of salvation that the
bread of life has come down from heaven to me.

That is the one point at which the Christian religion
is distinct from all the religions of the world. You can
go to the creeds of all the religions all over the world,
and they will give you as many steps to heaven as you
could possibly wish. If you follow these you are prom-
ised that you will get to heaven. But that is not good
news; we cannot climb to heaven.

Here is the good news of the gospel: the bread my
soul needs has come down. God does not say, 'There
you are; try to get yourself up to where I am.' No, he has

come down. The bread is the one who has come down from heaven (6:41). It is within our reach (Romans 10:6-8); all that we need in order to have our life transformed, our sins forgiven, peace with God, our conscience stilled, and to know absolute and complete pardon and forgiveness and reconciliation with God, is available.

There is no use, however, in bread being available unless it is actually eaten. The manna will not do any good on the wilderness floor: it needs to be gathered and taken in and consumed. It has to enter into the body. It is no use admiring it and observing it unless we eat it. It's not enough to be an expert on bread-making — that will not satisfy hunger. Nor is it enough to be an expert on digestion — that will not satisfy either. The bread must be taken and eaten.

Isn't this what drove the prodigal son to his father's house? With sanity came the realization that his father's servants had more than enough bread, while he perished with hunger. He goes back to his father with the thought of that spare bread. What happens? Does the father meet him and put a robe and a ring on him and give him a loaf? No, he kills the fatted calf. 'Give it all to him. Let him eat to his full because it is there for him.' Why should he perish?

Why should any of us be lost when Jesus is so near? Why shouldn't you be a Christian when the Word of God comes to you making the bread available? Have you never tasted that the Lord is gracious? He is available for us to take and to eat. Consume him like the bread that he is.

> ## The bread of heaven is free for us

Isaiah expresses this magnificently in his gospel call:

> Why do you spend your money for that which is
>   not bread,
>   and your labour for that which does not
>   satisfy?
> Listen diligently to me, and eat what is good,
>   and delight yourselves in rich food.
> Incline your ear, and come to me;
>   hear, that your soul may live
>
> (Isaiah 55:2-3).

How many people are there who are labouring for the food that perishes? It need not be; Jesus is saying in the gospel, 'Come to me, buy wine and milk without money and without price.'

He is there for the taking, having paid all that was necessary. He walked every path that needed to be walked so that he could be yours for the taking. Maybe we need an appetite for him. Maybe you need God to show you just how empty your life is without the Saviour so that you might come on the terms of his unconditional offer. You pay nothing. You give nothing.

'What must I do to be saved?' a man in the Bible asked. To that there is only one answer: 'Believe on the Lord Jesus Christ.' Heaven's bread was obtained at a great price, but it is offered at no price at all.

The bread of heaven is satisfying for us

One taste of this bread, and life will never be the same again. Taste and see that God is good (Psalm 34:8). To trust in him is to be blessed, and it is never to hunger. John picks up on this in the book of Revelation as he looks into heaven and sees God's people around the throne. The Lamb is feeding his people, and the voice from heaven says, 'They shall hunger no more.'

That is true now and for all eternity. To eat this bread is to live for ever; it is to be satisfied to the depth of our souls; it is to have our lives filled with the best things. There are many things that Satan parades before us in this world, with which he tempts us. We dabble with them; we taste them; we try them out — but they all leave us so empty, so disappointed, so frustrated. The tragedy is that we keep going back to them, even when we know the damage they cause and the emptiness they produce.

But here is something that gives real, lasting satisfaction. People come back to it because they know that it satisfies and fills and does something that no other spiritual food can do. There is surely nothing that can commend this bread to us more than the promise that if we have it, taste it and eat it, we shall be completely satisfied, and will yearn for nothing else!

If you are a Christian and you have drifted away from the Lord, and other things have become more attractive, you know that you need to repent and get back to the table to eat the bread that will satisfy.

Maybe you are not a Christian, but you wish you too could feast on Christ. Well, there is nothing in Jesus keeping you away, nothing in God's people keeping you away, nothing in the Bible keeping you away. Jesus says to come and join the feast.

To taste heaven's bread is to have something in the soul to whet the appetite for the marriage supper of the Lamb, when all of God's people will go into the heaven from which this bread came down, and they will feast for all eternity around the Lamb's table and on this living bread. What a glorious transformation there would be in our souls if we could feast on the living bread, on Christ in all his glorious fullness! He has the power to fill and satisfy still.

WHO ARE YOU, JESUS?

'I am the bread of life; whoever comes to me shall not hunger, and whoever believes in me shall never thirst.'

Questions for further study and reflection

1. What comparisons can be made between bread for the body and bread for the soul? (Deuteronomy 8:3; Psalms 34:8; 107:9; John 6:53-55).

2. Is there a connection between Jesus as the bread of life and the sacrament of the Lord's Supper? (Matthew 26:26; 1 Corinthians 11:23-24).

3. How do the parables which involve feasting help us to understand Jesus as the bread of life? (Luke 14:15-24; 15:11-32).

2.

JESUS THE LIGHT

I am the light of the world

John 8:12

There is a connection between this saying of Jesus and the immediate context of the Feast of the Tabernacles. In John chapter 7 we read that the Feast of Tabernacles, celebrating the wanderings of the Israelites through the wilderness in the Old Testament, had come to a conclusion. There were two great features of this feast that took place around the temple precincts.

The first was that every day the priest would take some water from the Pool of Siloam and pour it out beside the altar at the temple. This was a reminder that God had provided for his people in the desert; they had been given water to drink. This water imagery, together with the action of pouring it out, was highly significant.

Jesus' use of this, calling people to drink from himself, pointed forward to the gift of the Holy Spirit, the ultimate provision that Jesus was to make for his people. So we read:

> On the last day of the feast, the great day, Jesus stood up and cried out, 'If anyone thirsts, let him come to me and drink. Whoever believes in me, as the Scripture has said, "Out of his heart will flow rivers of living water."' Now this he said about the Spirit, whom those who believed in him were to receive, for as yet the Spirit had not been given, because Jesus was not yet glorified (John 7:37-39).

The other feature of the Feast of Tabernacles, as it was celebrated in Jesus' time, was the lighting of particular lamps in the temple; four great lamps were lit every evening, so that the temple was ablaze with light. At the close of the feast, one lamp was left unlit, symbolizing, in the thinking of the Jewish people, that full salvation had not yet come because the Messiah had not yet appeared.

Therefore, it is also significant that, as the Feast of Tabernacles comes to a close with that unlit candelabrum, Jesus should say, 'I am the light of the world.' In John's Gospel a clear connection is being drawn between Jesus' description of himself as the light of the world and the context of the festival in which this statement is made.

The theme of light in John's Gospel

But this is also a significant saying within the wider context of John's Gospel. In the prologue, the first eighteen verses of the Gospel, John emphasizes the deity of Jesus Christ. He was in the beginning. He was with God. He was God. He became flesh, and dwelt among us. He continues to be God and man; in addition to all that was true of him as God from all eternity, he has taken our nature to himself and in one person he unites the divine and the human. This is the Word which became flesh and tabernacled among us. John tells us that Jesus came down from heaven. We must believe that he is the Son of God.

John develops this theme: in him was life. Jesus exists independently of everything else that exists; that is why John says that he made all things, and without him nothing was made that was made (1:3). In other words, he was not made; he does not depend for his own existence on anything that has been made. In him is life, independent of everything else. Everything else that exists is dependent on him, while he is dependent on nothing.

John immediately tells us that the life in Jesus is the light of men. That is the light that shines in the darkness. That is the light of which John the Baptist spoke, as he bore witness to the light. He was not the light; he spoke about Jesus, preparing the way for him, blazing a trail for him, and now the true light comes into the world.

From the outset John has linked the being and the person and the glory of Jesus with the light that we need. It is a theme that he develops through the Gospel. We are not far into John's account when we read about the encounter of Jesus with Nicodemus, that great man who had so much, and yet had so little. He was in spiritual darkness. That is symbolized to a degree by the fact that he came to Jesus by night (3:2). Perhaps he wanted to disguise his meeting, or hide the encounter, yet the fact that it was night-time was also highly symbolic. Jesus goes on in chapter 3 to talk about the world being in darkness, about men loving the darkness rather than the light and about coming to the light (3:19-21).

Chapter 9 is going to tell us about a man born blind. His whole life is darkness. He cannot see or enjoy the benefits and blessings of the sun or its light. He was born blind. But Jesus is going to open his eyes. Jesus is to reveal to him the blessings of light.

We also read about Judas, at that great, solemn moment when Jesus has washed the feet of the disciples and is preparing for his appointed end. Satan entered into Judas, and he went out and, says John, 'it was night' (13:30). It was highly symbolic that he should go out into darkness, because the darkness was so much in him.

As John brings the Gospel to a conclusion, he reminds us of these great themes of night and day, light and darkness. The women come to the sepulchre early in the morning, when the shadows of night are about to give way to the rays of the dawn (20:1). The breaking of the light is symbolic of the light that has broken out of the darkness of the tomb, a light going to dawn on the women and the disciples and the whole world.

That night the disciples meet together, closed inside an upper room, afraid of the Jews. Yet light comes through with the appearing of Jesus. Again with the morning light they meet the risen Christ, the stranger on the shore.

Thus we are reminded throughout John's Gospel of the contrast between light and darkness, and now, at the centre of the Gospel, comes this great claim on the lips of Jesus: 'I am the light of the world.'

Light in the wider context of Scripture

So we must link this statement to the immediate context of the Feast of Tabernacles, and to the context of the Gospel of John as a whole, but we can also link it to the wider context of Scripture itself. What was the first thing God ever said? According to Scripture God's first words were, 'Let there be light' (Genesis 1:3). The first thing God did as he brought the world into being was to separate the light from the darkness.

That is where we begin in the book of Genesis: with God separating the light from the darkness. And that is also where we end in the book of Revelation. The same sovereign God distinguishes between light and darkness as he takes his people into the glory of heaven's city. There the inhabitants of that heavenly Jerusalem do not need the light of the sun or of the moon because this Jesus, the Lamb in the midst of heaven's throne, is the light of heaven for ever and ever (Revelation 21:23). They are in a place where their sun will never set and their moon will never be darkened. God will be their everlasting light. There they are bathed in heaven's light, and there is no shadow caused by this light. They have left the shadowlands behind, and they have gone into the land of perfect day and into the glory of heaven. The nations walk in this light.

But the last thing the sovereign Lord does is to separate the light from the darkness. There is a darkness outside of this city — the Bible calls it 'outer darkness' (Matthew 25:30) — in which there is no glimmer of light. That is the awfulness of this other destination of the human soul — a place where light does not penetrate, which is outside the city.

This is what makes the gospel so utterly solemn, so absolute and so important. We shall all, one day, spend eternity either in the light or in the darkness.

So, in the whole context of Scripture, we are dealing with a fundamental issue. Jesus addresses it in this unique claim: 'I am the light of the world.'

This light comes into the darkness

That is John's whole emphasis. In Jesus there is light, and it has come into our world. According to the words of our text, there is light in our dark world. There is the light of the gospel, the light of God's truth manifested in Jesus Christ. This is not a light that the world could ever have produced by itself, or for itself. It is not a light that could have come from any natural source. There is no energy in this universe that could have produced this light that the world needs. It had to come into the darkness from the outside.

It was not always the case that the world lay in darkness. At the very outset the light of God's own presence filled the world of Adam and Eve in that state of innocence in which they were created. They chose the darkness. They thought that by disobeying God they could add to perfection and have more than they possessed at that present moment. But it was the opposite. They lost everything.

Sin always produces a loss. Driven out of the garden, they — and we — were plunged into darkness. They could not get back to paradise, and they cannot get us back there either. There is no way back to Eden, no return route by which men and women can make it back to the paradise they have left behind. There is a sword of fire which bars the way, and they cannot retreat to that golden age now in their past. The world has now fallen into darkness, and there is no resource, no place in the whole of the sin-blackened universe, that can give man the light he needs.

But the glory of our text is that there is a light in this dark world, not because it has come from us, or from the world. It has come into the darkness from the outside. Isn't this amazing? Isn't this what the prophet said?

> The people who walked in darkness
>   have seen a great light;
> those who dwelt in a land of deep darkness,
>   on them has light shined
>
> (Isaiah 9:2).

John tells us elsewhere that God is light, and has no darkness in him (1 John 1:5).

The glory of the gospel is that the light that belongs to God has come into this world of darkness. The light of the gospel points us to the one who came, to the one who stepped into our darkness in order to save us. And how did he save us? He saved us by himself enduring the darkness that we brought in by the Fall. It was not without reason that when Jesus died at midday the world was shrouded in darkness. It was the very opposite of what happened at his birth. At that time there was supernatural light which transformed the midnight sky. Angels sang, and shepherds saw glorious light.

But when he died, darkness covered the world as he cried out, 'My God, my God, why have you forsaken me?' (Psalm 22:1; Matthew 27:46). He came right into our darkness, deliberately stepping into it, experiencing it in all its horror and terror. And he did this in order that there might be light for us.

For us, there is a problem with the human condition to which the answer lies outside of ourselves. All the gurus of the world have twisted the truth; the world has told us that the problem is outside and the solution within ourselves. Apparently all we need to do is to unlock our own potential, and get into our own resources and energies.

That is not what the Bible says. According to the Bible, the problem is absolutely within ourselves, and the solution is outside. Until we recognize this, we shall never know peace with God. The sin problem, the darkness problem, is in our hearts. The solution, thanks be to God, has come to us by God's grace from outside of ourselves. The light has come into the darkness.

| The light exposes the darkness |

It is the presence of the light in the world, in the person of Jesus Christ and his truth, that exposes just how dark the world truly is. You know what it is like to be sitting in your home at evening time. The shadows are lengthening, but you don't really notice it because you have been sitting there in the dusk.

Then the light comes on and momentarily blinds you! It makes you realize just how dark the evening has become. It was the light that really showed the measure of the darkness. That is how it was with Jesus too. The light came into the world, and immediately his presence exposed the darkness for what it was.

When we observe Jesus and follow him in his conversations with people, and in his interactions with them, we see how the light that is in him serves to reveal the darkness that is in them. B. B. Warfield has a tremendous little chapter in which he describes Jesus as 'the measure of all men'. He says:

> When we see Jesus, it must be in the brightness of his unapproachable splendour that we see those about him, just as it is in the light of the sun that we see the forms and colours and characters of all objects on which it shines. Especially when we see him in conflict with his enemies we cannot escape the spectacle of his utter perfection, and in that light the spectacle of the

utter depravity of men. Men are revealed in this presence in their true, their fundamental natural tones, with a vivid completeness in which they are never seen elsewhere.[1]

In other words, when Jesus came into the world, God let down a plumb line. If someone is building a wall, he needs to make sure that the wall is straight. So he allows the plumb line to drop. It is absolutely straight. Once it appears, then you can see how straight the wall is — not just by looking at it, but by measuring it against something that is truly straight. Jesus comes among men, the light of the world, and, in the light of his utter glory and splendour and perfection and light, you see the utter depravity of the human heart.

If you want to get the true measure of yourself, you must stand side by side with Jesus. It is no use standing side by side with another sinner, not even a religious sinner, or someone in the church, not even with a minister, or elder, or deacon, or any office-bearer. To see what you really are in your own heart, you need to stand next to Jesus.

The test is not what we are like in comparison with other people, no matter how religious they are. The test is what we are like beside him. What does the light in him say about the darkness in us? Warfield continues:

They cannot escape it. Against their wills they
are tried and tested every moment they live in
the presence of this Light... As he moves through
the world the whole race lies at his feet, self-
condemned. We shudder, as in the light of his
brightness we see man as he is.[2]

The very presence of the light exposes the darkness.
The life God wants is the life Christ lived. If our life can
measure up to his, God is pleased with us. But if there
is any point at which it does not, if there is one ounce
of darkness still in that heart, then God cannot accept
it, and will not accept it.

The light condemns the darkness

This is not how it ought to be with us. John says:

Whoever believes in him is not condemned,
but whoever does not believe is condemned already, because he has not believed in the name
of the only Son of God. And this is the judgement: the light has come into the world, and
people loved the darkness rather than the light
because their deeds were evil (John 3:18-20).

Does this describe our situation? Jesus stands before
us, exposing the darkness that makes us love sin and

self more than God, and the light condemns the darkness. We stand before God utterly without excuse, without plea, with no merit and no righteousness. Everything good about us is like filthy rags because his glorious perfect light condemns the fact that we have opted to walk away from the light.

In the presence of Jesus it is not just that we are seen to be darkness; it is that we are condemned for what we are. Guilt attaches to us. We have dishonoured God, and for that there is no excuse.

The light is in conflict with the darkness

John says elsewhere, 'If we say we have fellowship with him while we walk in darkness, we lie and do not practise the truth. But if we walk in the light, as he is in the light, we have fellowship with one another, and the blood of Jesus his Son cleanses us from all sin' (1 John 1:6-7). We need to walk in the light because we cannot have it both ways: we cannot have eternal life by walking in darkness.

There is a conflict between these two realities. Jesus is the light of a world in darkness. And what is that darkness going to do to the light? It is going to take him and crucify him. Up to this point in John's Gospel Jesus has been teaching the crowd, but now the crowd will be hostile, and will show just how much darkness is in them, to the extent that the people will say, 'Not this man, but Barabbas!'

There is ongoing conflict between the light and the darkness. That was vividly illustrated in the experience of the Israelites in Egypt. All the plagues that came upon the land of Egypt, as God said, 'Let my people go', were a preparation for the ultimate judgement — the death of the firstborn, moving towards the redemption of the people of God.

One of these plagues was a plague of thick darkness. Shrouded in darkness, people in the land of Egypt were paralysed. They could not get up off their beds; there was not a single ray of light, no glimmer at all breaking through. Mothers could not attend to their children; fathers could not attend to the needs of the household, because of the confining, blinding, disabling darkness that came upon them for their sins.

But the Israelites in the land of Goshen had light wherever they lived (Exodus 10:23). This world is all in darkness, but Jesus is the light. If we follow him, we shall not walk in darkness. Sin's darkness still disables, leaves us helpless and unable to work for the glory of God in all we do. The light is still in conflict with the darkness, warring against it. Those who follow Jesus are still in conflict with those who are in the darkness. Know the blessing of walking in the light and the blessing of his blood cleansing you. In John's words in the prologue, the darkness cannot extinguish, or overcome, this light (John 1:5).

The light can scatter the darkness

Paul describes the glory of the new birth in this way: 'God, who said, "Let light shine out of darkness," has shone in our hearts to give the light of the knowledge of the glory of God in the face of Jesus Christ' (2 Corinthians 4:6). God can dispel the darkness of the human heart to show us the glory of God. Peter explains the nature of the Christian life like this: 'But you are a chosen race, a royal priesthood, a holy nation, a people for his own possession, that you may proclaim the excellencies of him who called you out of darkness into his marvellous light' (1 Peter 2:9). This is what it means to be a Christian.

The psalmist expresses it like this: 'For it is you who light my lamp; the LORD my God lightens my darkness' (Psalm 18:28); 'The LORD is my light and my salvation; whom shall I fear?' (Psalm 27:1); 'The LORD is God, and he has made his light to shine upon us' (Psalm 118:27). That is the glory of the gospel. In him was life, and his life is the light of men.

As God's people journeyed through the wilderness, they followed that light, that pillar of fire, that glory presence. The book of Proverbs says that 'The path of the righteous is like the light of dawn, which shines brighter and brighter until full day' (Proverbs 4:18). It is not dull to be a believer! There will be many shadows crossing our path here in this world. But we walk in the light and are called to be children of the light.

God's people cannot always say that their path has been one of bright sunshine. But they can say that from the moment this light first shone into their souls, their experience has been one of sunlight in increasing measure. Even in spite of all the shadows and the long, lonely nights, they know that, while sorrow and mourning endure for a night, joy will come in the morning.

John sees the morning dawn with all the glory of resurrection power. That is why he would have made a connection between what he records of the women who came to the sepulchre as morning light was appearing and what he saw in the revelation of a new day dawning for the people of God, when God takes his people home to a place of perfect day, with no night there (Revelation 21:4; 22:5).

It is difficult to imagine a world with no more darkness, or sin, or sorrow, or pain, or lonely nights, or hard valleys, or long shadows. Those who have come into the glory of heaven, where the Lamb is the light, have heard him saying, 'I am the light of the world.' They have come to the light, and they love the light, and they walk in the light, and they have fellowship with one another, and his blood cleanses from all sin. Jesus, and no one else, is the light we need.

WHO ARE YOU, JESUS?

'I am the light of the world. Whoever follows me will not walk in darkness, but will have the light of life.'

Questions for further study and reflection

1. What was the ninth plague on Egypt, the plague of thick darkness, intended to teach God's people about the light of the world? (Exodus 10:21-23).

2. How does the contrast between light and darkness help us to understand the change that takes place when a person becomes a Christian? (2 Corinthians 4:6; Ephesians 5:8-10; 1 Thessalonians 5:4-5).

3. How does the reference to light in Revelation 22:5 compare and contrast with the references to light in the creation story? (Genesis 1:3-5,14-19). How does it help us to understand what heaven will be like?

3.

JESUS THE DOOR

I am the door

John 10:9

'I am the door,' is the third of the 'I am' sayings in John's Gospel. The context in which this statement was made by Christ follows on from the events recorded in the previous chapters, all of which take place around the conclusion of the Feast of Tabernacles in Jerusalem.

The Feast of Tabernacles was significant for the second of the 'I am' sayings — 'I am the light of the world.' As we saw in the previous chapter, at that feast there was a lot of light around the temple precincts, and on the last night there was one lamp, or candelabrum, which was left unlit to show that full salvation had not yet come. Against that background Jesus made the claim that he himself is the light of the world.

That claim was illustrated very vividly in the experience of the blind man in John 9. From birth his vision had been severely impaired, yet God restored his sight. Here was a man who was literally walking in darkness, and then the light of the world met with him and gave him light. One of the immediate effects of this was conflict, as the man found himself at odds with the religious leaders over the identity and the power of Jesus. There was a conflict between the light and the darkness; there is always a conflict between the light and the darkness.

In John 10 Jesus teaches explicitly that there is a great contrast between him and the religious leaders. Jesus contrasts himself with 'thieves and robbers'. The shepherd image of this chapter may well also be drawn from the Feast of Tabernacles, in which God's people were reminded of the way in which God shepherded his people through the wilderness. In this great shepherd chapter of the New Testament Jesus is linking himself into the history of Moses shepherding the people.

However, before he describes himself as the good shepherd Jesus says, 'I am the door.' We have already noted that there are no parables in John's Gospel. It is the case, however, that the word 'parable' is used in the Authorized (or King James) Version translation of John 10:6, to describe the language of Jesus. The ESV uses the term 'figure of speech'.

There is an analogy here between Jesus' teaching about himself and God as the shepherd of the sheep. It is not a parable in the sense of a story — the way that the other three Gospels use the term 'parable'; it is an analogy, an illustration. The Jewish people were familiar with the world of shepherding and looking after sheep. Jesus sheds light on his own ministry and message by means of an illustration.

Jesus is both the shepherd and the door

Jesus mixes his figures of speech here. Before he describes himself as the shepherd of the sheep, he describes himself as the door of the sheep. But even when you try to work out the significance of the door, you discover that the door is that by which the shepherd enters, in comparison with the robbers and the thieves who break in over the wall by some other way. There is a gatekeeper who allows the shepherd in. Jesus therefore is the shepherd, who is also the door.

So what is he saying? He is illustrating something with which his hearers, and perhaps also we as his readers, are familiar: when sheep are gathered they need to be gathered somewhere; they need to be enclosed in some kind of pen. They can wander about for a good part of the year, but there are other times when they need to be gathered in for one reason or another. They need to be secured and closed in.

In Palestine, the sheep would often be enclosed in an area that consisted simply of a wall with a gap in it. The shepherd himself would sometimes stand, or sleep, in that gap to keep the sheep in. Perhaps there might be several of these enclosures, with a 'door-keeper', or 'gatekeeper', looking after the different pens and the sheepfolds, so that each shepherd could then tend to the sheep.

So in one sense Jesus is the one who enters in by the door. He has legitimacy and authority to look after his sheep, and he does it well. He is the true shepherd, who knows his sheep. This will be explored later in the same chapter in the great teaching that Jesus is the good shepherd.

But, in another sense, Jesus can also claim to be the door. In its own way this is a powerful, vivid and important statement of what he is and does. Jesus is the one who guards and protects his sheep. By him, people can enter and be safe. At one level it is the most staggering claim in the whole world. This one, unique individual, the Jesus of the Gospels, is saying that in what he is and what he has done there is security for all who come to him.

Nobody else could make that claim. There is not one figure on the stage of human history who can speak in the way that Jesus speaks here. He is making the most absolute and ultimate statement of all. There is salvation for us, but it is in him alone. There is salvation for anyone, and it is in him. It is possible for anyone and everyone to come to him, as one would enter through a door, and find salvation.

So, even if we all came to Jesus at the same time, with all our sins, seeking salvation, we would find it in him immediately. He is the door. This is the Jesus of the gospel, offering, guaranteeing and pledging himself to us and for our safety. If we come to him through the door we shall be saved.

What is Jesus telling us when he says, 'I am the door'?

The door is a symbol of identity

It is often the case that you can identify a building by its door. In many ways the door is the first point of contact you have with the building. If you want to give someone directions to a house, you point them in the general direction of the village they are going to, and you tell them to count the doors and look for the house with this particular door. If they find that door they will be at the right place. The door identifies the house.

There are some famous doors, aren't there? A picture of a large, black door with the number 10 on it would identify itself (to British readers, at least) as the door of 10 Downing Street, the prime minister's dwelling. You wouldn't have to think very hard about it; the door behind which the prime minister resides and the government meets is so powerful an image that you can identify it easily. It is only a door, yet it identifies one of the most famous and most powerful buildings in the world.

Let me begin there. You identify salvation with Jesus. He is the door. He says that to enter by *him* is to have salvation. If you are looking for a salvation, but it doesn't have Jesus as the first point of contact, you are at the wrong door. And if you are at the wrong door, you are at the wrong house.

The tragedy is that so many people are looking for salvation, for emancipation — they need rest for their consciences and peace in their hearts; they want their lives to have direction and purpose and peace with God — but they are at the wrong door. You know you are at the right door if you have Jesus. Every aspect of his life, his death, his resurrection and ascension, and all that he does in heaven — that is what sinners need. I identify salvation by the door which is Jesus.

That has so many profound consequences in our lives and thinking. I must look away from myself to him. I must focus on him and look to him. At the beginning of John Bunyan's *Pilgrim's Progress* Christian comes out of the City of Destruction. He has a burden on his back, and he meets Evangelist, who explains to him something about his situation. He says, 'Do you see that gate? You make for it. Head for the wicket gate, and from there you will see the cross.' Spurgeon comments on that point in Bunyan and asks, why didn't Evangelist just point him directly to the cross? Why did he put the gate in between? People need to be directed to the cross. It is there for them. Send them to the cross!

I am not so sure that Bunyan was in fact preaching anything else, but the point is valid none the less. If we want to show people where salvation is to be found, we must send them straight to Jesus. We don't say to them, 'Make sure you are dressed properly first.' There are some houses to which you wouldn't want to come unless you were dressed in a particular way. You wouldn't want to cross the threshold unless you were well dressed.

But this door accepts everyone; it is for sinners that this Jesus came. I can go to him immediately and as I am. Whatever my past, present or future, whatever my situation, I can go to him now. Age doesn't matter and experience doesn't matter. Reformation of life doesn't matter. This Jesus came for sinners, and sinners can come directly to him. Anything else is not the salvation of the New Testament. Anything else is not the gospel of the New Testament.

If I identify this salvation with anything else, I have it all wrong. Whether that salvation is based on my good works, or my righteousness, or my obedience — if that is the basis of my acceptance with God, I have it all wrong. I know I must stand before God, and if my argument is that my life has been relatively decent, not a bad life, I have it all wrong.

It is not my spiritual experiences, or the nature of my testimony, or what moves me, or my feelings, that count. If these are the things with which I identify salvation, I have it wrong. It is not a particular set of creeds that saves — things I believe or subscribe to; it is not my Calvinism that will save me, or my grasp of reformed doctrine, or my knowledge of the Bible. These are not the things with which I identify this salvation. No, I must simply look to Jesus. He is the door. He is the frontispiece of the gospel. He is the one by whom I can identify God's salvation.

If I have a claim to salvation that is divorced from Jesus Christ, it is no salvation at all. It must be him — Jesus alone, in his glory and grandeur and finished work. Absolute salvation is guaranteed to me *in him*. If his person and work are the basis of my salvation, I have it all right.

The door is a symbol of access

'If anyone enters by me, he will be saved' (10:9). Now I know that Jesus also speaks in this verse about going in and out and finding pasture — he extends the imagery vividly — but the point is still clear. It is by entering *through* the door that a person is saved.

Could it be more simple or clear? By coming through this door, one is saved. There is no other door of which this is true — no other access, and no other way. Jesus is talking here in the most exclusive of terms. There is no other door into the kingdom, but there is a glorious door here.

The glory of this door is that it is not locked. It is not even closed. If the gospel is being preached, God's door gives us access. Perhaps the door of our heart is closed against Jesus. Perhaps he is not getting in. The beauty of the gospel, however, is that even though we may close our door against Jesus, he does not close his door against us. His door is wide open.

This door is here to give access. We open the doors of the church so that people will get in. We do not open them so that people will stand outside admiring the doors; we don't open them so that people will stay on the threshold. We open the doors so that people will enter. The door is the point of access to the building.

And here is Jesus saying the same thing to us: 'I am the door.' Are there people who are content to stand and marvel at the door? They just stand and look, with an interest in Jesus, but they have never crossed the threshold. They have admired his life, his death, his teachings, his examples — but they have never entered the building.

Jesus is saying that if he is the door, then he is there to give us access through himself into this salvation, and until we enter we cannot be in his kingdom. It is the same point that is made in the Sermon on the Mount: there is a narrow gate and a way which lead to life (Matthew 7:13-14). But what is the point of knowing this unless we enter the gate and walk the way?

I love Dr Martyn Lloyd-Jones' sermon on these words from Matthew. What is the narrow gate like? Lloyd-Jones says, 'I like to think of it as a turnstile. It is just like a turnstile that admits one person at a time and no more. And it is so narrow that there are certain things which you simply cannot take through with you. It is exclusive from the very beginning.'[1] Think of a football stadium. All these thousands of spectators come in through the turnstiles one by one. That is how the great company of the redeemed enter the kingdom of God — individually. They fill his house to overflowing, having entered the door one by one.

We enter churches this way. We don't let others enter for us; we take the step ourselves. Wasn't it like that for Noah and his generation? Noah heard God's word and built the ark. So there is a huge ark here, a huge floating box, and God has said that it is going to rain for forty days and forty nights. There isn't going to be any salvation anywhere; no one will be safe when God's judgement comes.

But the God of the judgement is also the God of grace; the God who sends the rain also sends the plan for the ark. The God who judges the world is the God who makes a way of salvation for Noah and his family, and that ark is only as good as the door. The ark is only as good as their entering into it. So the time comes when the flood is to be poured out, and it is not the building of the ark that is going to save Noah. The construction of this great boat is not what is going to keep the family safe. By faith he built the ark according to God's command, but God said to him, *'Go in!'*

So through the door he goes, and then he is within the security and safety of the ark. Where are we? Jesus says, 'I am the door.' Have we crossed this threshold? Maybe we have decided we are not good enough. But he does not keep out those who are not good enough! Those are the very ones he calls to come in!

He opens wide the door of salvation for sinners who are not good enough. He pleads with men and women and boys and girls to come in by the open door to Jesus. His shed blood and righteousness, his life, his death and his resurrection are the essence of the gospel, and we are called to go in by this door, and not by any other.

The door is a symbol of security

I think this is the most obvious point of the image here. There is security in Jesus, who guards the sheepfold. He stands in the gap so that the sheep are safe behind the door. When they come in for rest, they are safe. Even when they go out for pasture, he keeps his eye on them.

Let's return to Noah's ark. Is there not a magnificent moment in the story of Noah in Genesis 7 when the ark is ready, and the clouds are ready and God is ready? But before the judgement comes God tells Noah to enter the ark. So they go into it, and we read in the Bible that 'the LORD shut him in'. Now Noah is safe. Now he is secure. God shut him in.

When the children were small, it was easy to close up the house at night, to lock the door. They were all in bed and asleep. You could get off to bed at the end of the day. It was all so wonderful. Then they grew a little older, and started exerting their own independence. They weren't always back home when you wanted them; sometimes it was such a relief to hear the door closing, and to know they were in and were safe.

They didn't understand what you were worrying about. Of course they were safe! Why wouldn't they be? Nothing was going to happen to them! But they didn't have a parent's heart and concern and worry; perhaps one day they too will experience those long hours of worry in the night just waiting to hear the door close.

The Lord shut him in. There was safety and security there — everything was shut in behind the locked door. There is a Jesus in the gospel who says, 'I am the door.' You want to know you are safe? Your safety is just as good as your door. Your security is guaranteed by the strength of the door.

So Jesus says that everything he has done is guaranteeing the eternal security and salvation of everyone who puts their trust in him. That guarantee is under-scored in this chapter: 'They will never perish, and no one will snatch them out of my hand' (10:28). They are closed in with Jesus.

The psalmist expresses this thought: 'I am a so-journer with you, a guest, like all my fathers' (Psalm 39:12). What a marvellous concept! He doesn't say, 'I am a stranger *to* you,' but 'I am a stranger *with* you.' By nature we are strangers *to* God, but when you cross this threshold and enter this door and come into this sal-vation, instead of being a stranger to God, and a so-journer here without him, you become a stranger *with* God, and a pilgrim here in his company.

Where would Noah rather have been? To be closed in with God was his security. To be closed out from God was to face judgement and death. For all the discomfort and trials, for these long weeks of confine-ment he would rather be shut in by God and preserved and kept safe. If you are in Christ, there is nothing in life, or death, or in this world, or that to come, that can threaten your security (Romans 8:39). Who can separ-ate us from the love of Christ?

'Nothing!' is the answer! God's people are secure behind this door.

The door is a symbol of division

The same door that shut Noah in closed the world out. Have you ever gone somewhere and realized that you were too late? You got there, but the doors were closed. It's not a nice feeling. Yet the Lord takes up the image in Matthew 25:10, with the wedding feast to which people came, but the doors were shut.

The same doors which closed some in to the banquet closed others out. Isn't that what happens when you close the doors of your house at night? You shut the family in and the world out. That door becomes the most powerful symbol of division at that point in your life.

I think Jesus is capturing that also. 'I am the door,' he says. There is salvation, and you identify it with him. There is access to it by him. There is security behind this door. But the same door that closes his people in to the glory of this salvation closes others out.

What matters supremely is the side of the door you are on. Do you know him? Have you come to find pasture and salvation in him? Can you say with the psalmist in Psalm 118:20, 'This is the gate of the LORD; the righteous shall enter through it'? There is the sound of salvation where the righteous dwell. Do we sing this song? Do we know we are saved by trusting in his finished work at Calvary?

The door is open, but it still divides. Jesus says, 'Come, for everything is ready,' but it won't always be like this. One day he will close the door, and it will matter supremely which side of the closed door we are on. When the flood comes, it isn't the kind of life we have lived, or the kind of people we have been, or how often we went to church or read our Bibles, that will matter, but what side of the door we are on.

Am I saying that will be what matters then? No! It is what matters right now. Where are we in relation to him? If we have come in, we are safe. If we are lingering outside, we are not. What a blessing that he still offers this salvation! May we all know it just by crossing this threshold!

WHO ARE YOU, JESUS?

'I am the door. If anyone enters by me, he will be saved, and will go in and out and find pasture.'

Questions for further study and reflection

1. What are the implications of the Lord shutting Noah into the ark? (Genesis 7:16). Why did God not leave it to Noah to close the door? What can we understand about the nature of salvation from the fact that it was God who closed the door?

2. How do you understand the prayer of Psalm 118:19 in the light of Jesus' teaching that he is the door to salvation?

3. Why is the door of salvation said to be 'narrow' in Matthew 7:13?

4. If Jesus is the door to heaven, in what sense could Peter be given the keys? (Matthew 16:19).

4.

JESUS THE SHEPHERD

I am the good shepherd

John 10:11

This is the fourth of the 'I am' sayings in John's Gospel, and the second to appear in chapter 10. We noted in our last study that the 'I am the door' saying is of a piece with the image and the analogy running through this section, with its idea of gathering sheep together and giving them security. The shepherd himself guards the entrance and is the door.

The image is extended in the familiar words of our text where Jesus calls himself the good shepherd. This is an image that runs through Scripture. One of the best-known psalms contains the words: 'The LORD is my shepherd; I shall not want' (Psalm 23:1). In other psalms the same metaphor appears: Psalm 80 describes

God as the 'Shepherd of Israel'; Psalm 77 describes him
as leading his people out of Egypt like a flock.

God always was the shepherd of his people. This is
one of the images that emphasize the uniqueness of
the relationship between God and his people. It appears in many different ways throughout the Scriptures. There is a relationship here which is unique and
unbreakable. *We* are his flock if he is our shepherd.

Before we come to look at the substance of this
claim, let's look at its significance. How significant is it
that Jesus should describe himself in this way? I think
it tells us one or two things about him.

It illustrates the kind of teacher that Jesus was

To have listened to Jesus was to have been taught the
highest concepts through the simplest of images.
Everyone who heard Jesus knew about sheep and
shepherding. Jesus is drawing on that familiar world of
caring for the sheep and shepherding the flock to bring
home to his hearers the most absolute and fundamental and glorious of all doctrines.

Isn't it the case that a good teacher will use the
simplest of illustrations to teach the most complex
concepts? There are things that are difficult to grasp
and are not immediately understood, yet a good
teacher will bring us gradually into an understanding

of the unfamiliar using these stepping stones of familiar realities.

Jesus was exactly this kind of teacher, and we are privileged to be taught by him. Part of his function as mediator is to fulfil the office of prophet. He is still a teacher. In this claim he is taking the familiar — the whole idea of shepherding — and he is teaching us the most glorious things about himself.

In this verse, for example, he takes us from the world of shepherding into the very heart of the atonement. We resonate with the image of the good shepherd, but look at where he runs with it: the good shepherd lays down his life for the sheep. So it is a great privilege to sit at the feet of so great a teacher.

It tells us about Jesus' relationship to the Bible

This concept tells us not just about the kind of teacher he is, but about the textbook he uses. There are other passages of the Bible which use the same image. Isaiah, Ezekiel, the Psalms and many other Old Testament passages feed their doctrines into this passage. The Old Testament is full of the doctrine that the Lord Jehovah searches for his sheep, carries his sheep and pastors his sheep.

All this Old Testament material is being poured into this claim on the lips of Jesus. It is impossible to do justice to the person and work of Christ without the

Old Testament. When the apostles preached the gospel, the Old Testament was all they had. But it was sufficient for them at that point. They took the Old Testament, with its prophecies, insights and doctrines, and they preached Jesus to the people.

They showed how the Old Testament was longing for and waiting for one to come who would fulfil all these prophecies and promises in the glory of his own work. But no one in the in the Old Testament could ever say, 'It is fulfilled now.' Here is Jesus placing a capstone on all these shepherd passages, these shepherd strands of Old Testament revelation, all culminating in his glorious person. He is the good shepherd.

So we take up the Old Testament because it tells us about him. We are not just New Testament Christians, but whole-Bible Christians, who want to use the whole Bible, the book Jesus used. We want to see Jesus, not just as the subject of New Testament stories and doctrines, but as the object of the Old Testament longing and anticipation, prediction and prophecy. The movements of history of which the Old Testament speaks are all pointing to him. So here Jesus is telling me about the importance of the Old Testament.

It is full of the doctrine of the divinity and deity of Jesus

That may not be obvious at first reading. When we read that Jesus is the good shepherd perhaps we just think of him drawing on the parallel with other shepherds. But let's think about it for a moment.

What was the Old Testament emphasizing? Who was the Shepherd of Israel? Who was it that led his people out of Egypt like a flock? Who guided them and guarded them in the wilderness? Who committed himself to Israel? None other than Jehovah God.

Ezekiel 34:15 makes it explicit: 'I myself will be the shepherd of my sheep..., declares the Lord GOD.' This is God speaking. This is no ordinary mortal. The Shepherd of Israel is Jehovah, the everlasting God. Now there is one standing before us in the redemptive drama of history and in the pages of the Gospels, and he is able to say, 'I am the good shepherd.'

Everything the Bible ever said about God is true about Jesus. When he makes this claim he is identifying himself with the Lord of the Old Testament, and there is no other. There is no shepherd but Jesus. There is no God but Jesus. There is no sovereign Jehovah but Jesus.

John is driving forward that doctrine. It is the very reason for his writing. He tells us that he writes in order that we might believe that Jesus is the Messiah, the Son of God (20:31). In John 10:19 he says that there was a division among the Jews because of Jesus. Of course there was a division — they knew their Bibles! They knew what Jesus was claiming when he said, 'I am the good shepherd.' They knew he was identifying himself with the God they worshipped, the God of whom their Scriptures spoke, and it was offensive to them. In verse 33 they say that they will stone him for blasphemy! He is a man, yet he makes himself God!

Yet he is God, incarnate, in the flesh. The Jesus of the Gospels is the Jesus that we worship. I know that intellectually the whole concept of the Trinity is difficult: Father, Son and Holy Spirit, yet there is only one God — not three different Gods, but one — three persons in the Godhead. Here is the Christian name of God: Father, Son and Holy Spirit. This is what the Bible teaches us. God is my Shepherd, my Jehovah, my Jesus.

So when Jesus says, 'I am the good shepherd,' it is of great significance. It teaches us about the teacher, the textbook and his subject — the divinity that belongs to him.

The good shepherd lays down his life for the sheep

So what is the substance of his claim to be the good shepherd? Let me emphasize the qualification 'good'. He is not just the shepherd, but the *good* shepherd. The importance is to be seen in this: the good shepherd is the one who lays down his life for the sheep. If you wish to see how good a shepherd he is, you must watch him as he goes to Calvary.

If you want to see the kind of shepherd that speaks here, follow him as he takes his long, lonely journey that will see him at last laying down his life. If you want to appreciate what this claim is saying, then take a look at Jesus in every stage of his life, and at last in his death and resurrection. Don't lift your eyes from him: watch him as he lives among men and teaches and moves towards the cross. He does nothing to avoid the cross; he sets his face like a flint towards Jerusalem; he hands himself over to those who will bind him to that cursed tree. What is he doing? At Calvary he is laying down his life. And why is he doing that? Because the giving of his life is going to benefit his flock.

That is how good a shepherd he is. He goes all the way to the cross, and at the cross the shepherd becomes the lamb, sacrificed to take away the sin of the world. That theme has been running through the Gospel from the outset, where John the Baptist preached him as the Lamb of God who takes away the sin of the world. He came to die at Calvary, to go to the cross, to lay down his life for these sheep. That is the measure of the goodness of this shepherd — what happens at Calvary.

So let's keep the cross before us as we look at this claim of Jesus. What shall we say about the one who says, 'I am the good shepherd'?

The good shepherd finds his sheep

He went to Calvary to lay down his life for those who were completely unlike himself, those who were far from God. He was never far from God. He was always close to God. He and his Father are one. They have communion. He was in the beginning with God (John 1:1-2). But he laid down his life for those who were far from God.

There is a powerful sheep image in the book of Isaiah — the prophet says that 'All we like sheep have gone astray' (Isaiah 53:6). That is where we are. We have wandered from the fold and, like sheep, we have followed one another into the paths of sin, far from God.

But this shepherd laid down his life in order to save his sheep. Isn't that what the parable of Luke 15:1-7 teaches so magnificently? The shepherd leaves the ninety-nine to find the lost sheep. It cannot wander back as it wandered away, or make its way into the fold as it made its way out of it. But there is a shepherd here. There is one who gave his life precisely in order to search out the sheep that was lost.

That means that if you are a Christian, it wasn't that you found Jesus, but that Jesus found you. Of course there is a sense in which we find Christ, but an even deeper sense still in which he finds us. The poet said:

I sought the Lord and afterward I knew
He moved my heart to seek him, seeking me;
It was not I that found, O Saviour true.
No, I was found by thee.[1]

This shepherd searches out and finds the lost sheep. What is he doing in the gospel? Why has Jesus commissioned the preaching of the gospel? Why does he send out preachers? He supplies the answer: the Son of Man came to seek and to save the lost! That is why he came, and it is what he is still doing.

That is why the gospel is so glorious. There is nothing more wonderful than to be where Jesus is passing by and searching out the sheep that are lost. That is what Jehovah had said in the Old Testament: 'I, I myself will search for my sheep and will seek them out' (Ezekiel 34:11). That note of grace sounds throughout the whole Bible. Why are people saved? It is not because of anything they have done, or their righteousness, or their good works, or their knowledge. It is simply because of the amazing grace of God: 'I once was lost, but now am *found.*'

That is the testimony of all of God's people, brought into the glory of his presence. They will sing to the praise of the glory of the grace that searched them out.

The good shepherd feeds the sheep

That is the pledge God made; he said that he would gather the sheep in order to feed them: 'I will bring them out from the peoples and gather them from the countries, and will bring them into their own land.

And I will feed them on the mountains of Israel'
(Ezekiel 34:13).

He feeds his sheep on the food that he secured for
them by laying down his life. He feeds his sheep on the
glories of Calvary's atonement. He brings them into
the covenant, out of the wilderness and into the fold.
He makes them part of his flock, providing for them
the best of fare, all that their souls need.

He feeds them constantly. He makes sure they are
nourished and provided for. There is nothing that
these sheep need that he has not secured for them
through his death on the cross. They lie down on good
grazing land. He leads them by still waters and in
green pastures and restores their souls.

The good shepherd protects his sheep

This flock is exposed to all kinds of dangers and
enemies. There are wolves and bears about, and the
sheep are so vulnerable. There is not one sheep in
Christ's flock who would say anything else. Every one
of them is open to the assaults of the enemy of their
souls, and the snares and temptations of the world,
exposed to the destructive power of sin and the assaults of this fallen world. But the good shepherd who
died for them protects his flock.

They are not going to come to any harm as long as
he is watching them. They commit their all to him. We

were like sheep going astray, says Peter, but now we have returned to the shepherd and bishop, or overseer, of our souls (1 Peter 2:25). So we have come to the shepherd, and he is the one who keeps his eye on his sheep. He has a pastoral function — the word 'pastor' is just the Latin word for a shepherd, and Jesus is the pastor of his flock. He protects them.

If we are in his flock we have every assurance that nothing will harm us, either in this world or in the world to come. Nothing out of hell will harm us — nothing at all, because his eye is on his flock.

The good shepherd cares for his sheep

They have not all reached the same place. They are not all on the same level. Some are strong; others are weak. Some of them are straying. Some are timid; some are fearful — there are all kinds of sheep here. Jesus cares for them all.

Isn't it glorious how God puts it? 'I will seek the lost, and I will bring back the strayed, and I will bind up the injured, and I will strengthen the weak... I will feed them in justice' (Ezekiel 34:16). Isaiah expresses it beautifully: the shepherd carries the lambs in his bosom and looks after those who are heavy with young (Isaiah 40:11). He knows all about the situation they are in, and he knows them personally. He gives them all his undivided attention, and lavishes on them the personal care they need.

All of this is poured into this claim: 'I am the good shepherd.' When he laid down his life, he showed how much he is bound to his flock. Having demonstrated what a great shepherd he is, he will continue to pour out on his people the riches of his grace. When you need him, he will be there. In all the different situations of your life, he will play the part of the shepherd, and you will be able to say, 'I shall not want.'

The good shepherd leads his sheep

He goes before them, leading them through the wilderness. He has a destination in view; in God's house for evermore their dwelling place will be (Psalm 23:6). This shepherd takes his sheep home, taking them not just to a barn, or a little outhouse beside his home. He is going to take them *home*. He laid down his life for them to secure them an eternal portion in his Father's house.

What a contrast there is between what they once were — lost and astray — and what they are going to be when he takes them all the way to glory and makes them like himself! Are we part of that journey? Are we following the shepherd, listening to his voice, as this chapter says? The sheep hear him, and they follow him. He says none will snatch them out of his hand. Are we on that journey?

Finally, this shepherd is going to come again to judge the world. When he does, when the Father commits all judgement to the Son, he will divide men and women as a shepherd divides sheep from goats, because he is going to separate his sheep, and will make the division between those who are his and those who are not.

One day the good shepherd will appear as the great shepherd and as the final, ultimate judge of all. Everything hinges on our relationship to the shepherd, because he will separate his flock. They will go with him when all the rest will be banished from his presence for ever.

It is a solemn business. He is the good shepherd who gave his life so that his people will be with him. Those who are not his will be separated into a lost eternity. Do we know the shepherd? There is nothing to compare with having him as our Lord and Saviour. Am I in his flock? Do I know his voice? Am I in his hand? He gave his life for us; may God grant that we return to him as to the shepherd and bishop of our souls!

WHO ARE YOU, JESUS?

'I am the good shepherd. The good shepherd lays down his life for the sheep.'

Questions for further study and reflection

1. What are the characteristics of the flock of Jesus? (John 10:26-28; 1 Peter 2:25).

2. In Isaiah 53, both we (v. 6) and the Saviour (v. 7) are described in terms of sheep. What points of comparison and contrast can we gather from this about ourselves and Jesus?

3. How is the image of Jesus the lamb and Jesus the shepherd combined in Revelation 7:17?

4. What adjectives and characteristics of Jesus as shepherd are brought out in the following verses: John 10:14; Hebrews 13:20; 1 Peter 5:4?

5.

JESUS THE RESURRECTION

I am the resurrection and the life

John 11:25

This is the fifth of the 'I am' sayings in John's Gospel. These sayings are unique to this Gospel, and each one of them reminds us of the glory of Jesus as the great I AM. The name of Jehovah is the name that Jesus appropriates to himself and fills out its meaning for us in the seven 'I am' sayings.

This fifth saying is a remarkable statement; these are familiar words set in a well-known context in the home at Bethany and in connection with the death and subsequent raising of Lazarus. Jesus is coming towards the end of his public ministry, and the opposition against him is growing. There is a great deal of conspiracy afoot to capture Jesus. That is clear at the end of the chapter, where we read about the intrigue of the Pharisees at the time of the Passover. They wonder whether Jesus will appear at the feast.

It is also captured for us in the comment Thomas makes when Jesus tells them that they are going to Bethany. Thomas says, 'Let us also go, that we may die with him.' Thomas realizes that for them to come out of relative obscurity and go to Bethany, nearer Jerusalem, is to walk a path fraught with danger. Thomas is saying, 'Yes, we might as well all go; then we shall all be dead!'

So there is a great deal of opposition to Jesus. Yet, remarkably, it is in that context that Jesus is going to perform his greatest miracle on that side of the cross. Before he goes to Calvary, and before the miracle of his own resurrection, he is going to perform another miracle to demonstrate his glory: he will bring Lazarus out of the grave. It is in this context that Jesus will make his great claim to *be* — not just to bring — resurrection and life.

Let's remind ourselves of one or two things in this passage.

This was a family that loved Jesus

Let's think for a moment about this particular home in Bethany, where Martha, Mary and Lazarus were. There were no children; none of them had married; they lived together — and they loved the Lord Jesus Christ. They gave him hospitality and a welcome when few places did. As soon as this cloud of sorrow and darkness came over their home, the sisters immediately sent word to Jesus. They sent the message that Lazarus, whom Jesus loved, was ill.

They were a family who loved Jesus. Theirs was a home where Jesus received a welcome. As soon as trouble came into their home, they immediately knew that the best thing to do was to take it to Jesus.

I think, even at this level, the home at Bethany shines on the pages of the Gospel as an example to our own homes and families. Is our home a home that welcomes Jesus? Is our home one that has a place for him? Is our family circle one where Jesus is honoured, respected and obeyed? Is it one where, if trouble arises, we know exactly where to go with it? Do we instinctively know that we can take our needs — not just individually, but as families — all to Jesus?

Is our home one where God's Word is honoured and God's Christ is welcome and God's cause is loved and God's people find a reception? In this world, where so few homes are hospitable to the Lord of glory, is our home a Bethany home? Is our family a Bethany family?

What about you young people out there — who are perhaps coming into years of responsibility and maturity and thinking about engagement and marriage and setting up a home — what kind of home do you want to have? You want a home full of love, joy and happiness, and these things are good. But I hope you have a Bethany home. I hope you set up a home where Jesus is always welcome and by his Spirit is always present. Perhaps you have recently been married and are setting out together on life's course. Is this your kind of home? Is this Jesus prayed to and honoured and worshipped in your family life? Does he have a place of primacy in your life? Do you love having Jesus round to visit? It's the best way to start out on married life together, to make sure your home is a Bethany home. Shining through this chapter is the remarkable place Jesus had in the affections of this home.

> *It was also a home that Jesus loved*

This was a place where Jesus came, because he needed friends and companions, and he enjoyed the fellowship of this home and he loved Martha and Mary and Lazarus. I think this is one of the great chapters in the Bible which stress for us the sheer glory of the humanness of our Lord.

Jesus loved this family. We are told this explicitly in verse 5. In verse 11 he calls Lazarus 'our friend'. In verse 36, when Jesus wept at his grave, the Jews remarked on Jesus' love. It was so obvious — Jesus loved this family and drew near to them at this time for this very reason. Perhaps more remarkable still is the fact that this chapter, which shows us the human Jesus, is also going to show us the supernatural Jesus whose glory is such that he can stand before the grave of Lazarus and say, 'Lazarus, come out.'

At one level, Jesus is so remarkably like us, but at another level he is so very different from us. His human emotions come through in this chapter. Lazarus was his friend. He was bound to him in ties of deep friendship and in a bond of fellowship that left him weeping over Lazarus' death.

It's good to have good friends. Our Saviour had good friends, and was himself a good friend to those whom he loved. He did not call Lazarus to be one of his apostles — don't you think that Lazarus would have made a good apostle? Don't you think that Lazarus would have been able to speak about things that Jesus can do for people in a way that none of the others could? He could have gone out and told others that he had died and been raised — but that was not his calling. His calling was just to be the friend of Jesus where he was, in that home in Bethany. He was not an apostle, not the author of any New Testament book, but in the relative obscurity of Bethany he was a faithful friend of Jesus, and Jesus loved him.

I think that is wonderful, because it is the calling of so many whom Jesus calls his friends. 'You are my friends,' he says, 'if you do what I command you.'

> *They learned much more about Jesus when trouble came*

When the dark clouds of death and separation came over their home and their family, they discovered more about Jesus than they could possibly imagine, and they found him in places and in ways in which they never expected to find him, seeing things they would never have seen had it not been for the death of Lazarus.

Isn't it amazing how many times Jesus speaks to us through things that are taking place in our lives, and in the life of our family and home? He uses children to speak to parents; he uses parents to speak to children, brothers to speak to sisters, and sisters to brothers. Sometimes God's voice is heard by us in things we would never have wished for, and would never have wanted to come into our homes and families. The sisters ran to Jesus; both said the same thing: 'If you had been here, my brother would not have died.' How they loved their brother! They would have given anything to have had him back with them again.

How often had they visited neighbours and friends when they had lost loved ones? How often had they mourned with others? Now it was their time to mourn. Now what they had seen so often in the homes and lives of families around them came to themselves. Let's never forget that there is a time for rejoicing and there is a time for weeping. The Bible reminds us that sorrow clouds can quickly come across our sky and blot out our sun; they can quickly bring unpleasant and difficult things into our lives; yet we are also reminded that through these things the Lord reveals himself as the Lord of life and of grace and of glory.

There are people reading this who can look back over their lives and see things written into their story that they would never have chosen for themselves, but they would also say that they would not have left these things out of their lives either. The Lord's way is always best. Even through pain and difficulty and darkness, Jesus makes himself known.

Their faith was tested by Jesus' delay

The message came in the first instance: 'Lazarus is ill.' Then the sisters sent word that 'Lazarus is dead.' There is delay on the part of Jesus; he waits before he acts — so much so that by the time he finally comes to Bethany, Lazarus is buried. 'If you had been here...', they say to him. 'If ... then...' 'If you had come earlier, then our brother would still be alive. If you had not delayed, things would be so different.'

But there is a song that says that, although Jesus was four days late, he was right on time. His timing in our lives is not always our timing. His timetable is not always the same as ours; sometimes there is good reason for him to delay. Sometimes he just wants us to exercise our faith with patience in the testing, knowing that he knows, and it is in his control. The sisters were probably right: if he had come earlier things would have turned out differently. But the reason he delayed was so that they would discover things they could otherwise never have known.

Maybe you are wondering what Jesus is doing with your life; maybe you have been praying, but there is no answer; maybe there are things that have concerned you over many years, but there is still no resolution. Maybe he has kept you waiting, and nothing seems to be happening — but in his own time it will be to his glory. That is what he said at the beginning.

Finally he comes, and Martha runs out to meet Jesus. It is so much in character — Martha just runs to Jesus, after hearing that he had come. She says that he could have prevented Lazarus's death — and so he could have. But Martha has to learn things about Jesus. 'Your brother will rise again.' Immediately Martha assumes that Jesus is speaking about the ultimate, final resurrection. 'I know he will rise on the last day,' she says. It is at this point that Jesus makes the claim: 'I am' — even now — 'the resurrection and the life.'

Let me say three things about these words.

These words are spoken by a remarkable person

This point hardly needs to be proved, but it is worth making none the less. There is no one like Jesus. One of the things that show me the uniqueness of Jesus is the fact that he can utter these words. No one else can. None of the disciples could have said them; the sisters of the dead man could not have said them; no one in the company could have said them. The high priest and the religious leaders could not speak like this. Only Jesus could say, 'I am the resurrection and the life.'

He is not saying that Martha is right to believe in the resurrection; nor is he saying that he himself believes and teaches the final resurrection; he says, 'I *am* the resurrection.' Combined in this unique person on the pages of John's Gospel is everything that is true of our humanness — Jesus weeps, groans, loves, comes with a heart full of affection for this family — and everything that belongs to the great I AM, to the great God that he is.

He combines in his person all that is true of God and all that is true of man. He can articulate the words that alone can address this situation: 'I am the resurrection and the life.'

There is no God but Jehovah, and Jehovah is Jesus, and stands alone on the pages of the Bible and on the stage of human history. His equal is found nowhere. This is unprecedented and unparalleled. You will not find another Jesus on the pages of the history books. The one who says, 'I am the resurrection,' is alone qualified to speak in this way, and there is nobody like him. That is why it is so important that we find him and close in with him, and make him our friend.

What a privilege — that they could claim this person as their friend; that he could say, 'our friend Lazarus'! This unique person has so much love for this family that their situation moves him to tears. 'We do not have a high priest who is unable to sympathize with our weaknesses,' says the New Testament. Do you think Christ is so remote that he doesn't know what you are going through? He was tempted in all points, but was sinless. His heart beat with the deepest affection. He groaned when he saw what death had done. He has been here, and he knows the trauma and difficulty of living in a fallen world. Yet as a man among men he is alone, the God-man, the great I AM. We worship him and follow him and say, 'To whom shall we go?' We say, 'No one ever spoke like this man.' He has words full of grace.

Is your ear tuned in to the voice of Jesus? His sheep hear his voice, and there is no one they wish to follow but him. His word fills, thrills and delights the soul. 'Whom have I but you alone?' He is absolutely unique. These words are the words of a remarkable person.

These words are full of remarkable power

They indicate for us that this Jesus has a power that no one has. It is not just that he has insight, understanding, sympathy and fellow-feeling that no one else has; this Jesus has a power that belongs to none other.

That is easily demonstrated; Jesus' power in this place is greater than the greatest power known among men. What is that? It is here — don't you see it here, in the cold, unfeeling tomb in which Lazarus is laid? Don't you see it in this separation and sadness and burden of grief that weighs this family down? The greatest power at work in the world is at work here — it is the power of death, the power that cuts right across all our dreams, hopes and aspirations. It is able to cause havoc and destruction and pain in human life.

Don't you see death waiting here to claim one after another of the lost, fallen sons of Adam? By one man's disobedience sin came into the world — and death by sin. Riding on the back of our rebellion is this power of death that comes with all its force and potency ripping through the resolutions and plans of people. We brush it aside and fail to give it the thought we ought to give it. We walk over the graves of others and fail to re-member that one day the place that knows us now will know us no more. We carry others to their last resting place, as Lazarus was carried and entombed behind that stone, and we forget that one day the same power will claim us also.

Does the Bible not say that it is appointed to us all once to die, and after death the judgement? There is no going beyond that boundary that God has set for our lives. We are made for eternity, and we are living in a world of sin and of death. It is so powerful. No one can say to death, 'Don't come here.' No one can say,

'Don't come here yet.' No one can say, 'Don't come here that way.' No one can say, 'Don't come here until...'

No, the power of death sweeps right across our human experience, and comes right into our homes and our lives. We must all sleep the sleep of death. Remember the powerful Old Testament image: 'We are like water spilled on the ground.' Try to gather it again — it is impossible. We live our lives like a tale that is told; then the power of death brings it all to an end and concludes the story in God's time, not in ours, according to God's appointment, not according to our plans.

Yet here is Jesus, in the face of the greatest power at work in human history, standing before it and saying, 'I am the resurrection.' Can you imagine the impact of that moment? Conscious as she is of the power that has carried her brother away, Martha is face to face with Jesus, and he is claiming a power greater than that of death. He is claiming to have the power of resurrection and the power of life in his own being and in his own person, and ultimately in his work.

That is why he stands alone, and why we must listen to him. Yes, our lives must go the way of all flesh. Yes, our lives will be spilled like water on the ground. Yes, we must leave this place and go into eternity. But let us listen to the one who has the keys of death in his hands, who can defy death and say, 'O death, where is your sting? O grave, where is your victory?'

This is the Jesus who can come with all the power of resurrection life and victory into hearts that are dead in trespasses and sins. He is not saying, 'I will be the resurrection on the last day,' but 'I am *now* the resurrection.' All those who are believers in the Lord Jesus have experienced the power of resurrection. The New Testament describes the new birth as a passing from death to life — that is resurrection. Jesus has come into the lives of men and women with unique resurrection power. He makes them alive. All that he does for his people by his grace in conversion is an act of resurrection. If we are born again we have been made alive spiritually. There is no life apart from him. Outside of him there is only sin and death. But his power brings the power of life into human experience.

This power is able to raise the dead when they hear the voice of the Son of God. This Jesus can do for you spiritually what he did for Lazarus physically — he can take you out of a grave of spiritual death into newness of life. No one else can do that. That is why he says, 'Seek me and live.'

> These words hold out a remarkable promise

What is the promise of these words? 'Your brother will live again.' Yes, Martha is right — he will rise on the

last day, but Lazarus, by a unique act of God's provi-
dence, is going to come out of the grave, and will
experience a reviving and a reconstituting of his
person; he is going to speak with them and sit with
them and eat with them. The foolish thing was that the
Jewish leaders, when they saw how people believed in
Jesus as a result of this miracle, said, 'Let's put Lazarus
to death!' Didn't they realize that if they put Lazarus to
death Jesus could raise him again? But sin is so blind to
all that Jesus does; here Jesus speaks into the teeth of
death and its power and pain — because of what Jesus
is, Lazarus will live again.

And Jesus continues to speak into the reality of
death and to hold out the promise that one day those
who sleep in him will be raised incorruptible and he
will change their vile bodies and make them like his
own.

That is the Christian hope — that death does not
have the ultimate word, or the final word. Death brings
many things to an end, but the power of him who is
the resurrection means that for all of God's people life
has the last word. All who are in their graves will hear
the voice of the Son of God, and those who hear will
live.

I cannot imagine that day; it defies my power of
imagination, but I believe it because I commit to the
promises Jesus makes to me, and he says, 'You will rise
again.' Jesus promises me that this world is just a
temporary place, a tent which one day will dissolve,

and we shall return to our constituent elements. We shall sleep the sleep of death, but it will not be for ever. The years will roll, and the centuries will see these bodies united to Jesus, and history will run its course; over these graves the world will carry on all its activities and carry out all its plans; but underneath that covering of dust the bodies of God's people will rest until the resurrection.

When that day dawns, and the trumpet sounds and the voice of the archangel summons God's people out of their graves for ever, there will be a resurrection and they will discover personally what it is to rise with triumph and place their foot on the neck of the enemy and see Jesus face to face.

Do you have that hope? There is nothing more important than that you should be able to know that when you die you will sleep in Jesus in the hope of the resurrection that belongs to those who trust in him.

But there will be another resurrection, of those who are not in Christ. They will be summoned to the bar of his final judgement. The Bible says little about it except that their resurrection will be a step towards the lost eternity that they chose for themselves in their rejection of Jesus. Make sure that, when the curtain finally falls, and when Jesus comes or calls, you are trusting in him who is the resurrection and the life. Then, with triumph and victory, you will be caught up into the clouds to meet the Lord in the air, on that day when Jesus shuts his people in and his enemies out.

'I am the resurrection and the life' — but is he our hope of resurrection and glory?

WHO ARE YOU, JESUS?

'I am the resurrection and the life. Whoever believes in me, though he die, yet shall he live, and everyone who lives and believes in me shall never die. Do you believe this?'

Questions for further study and reflection

1. How important is the resurrection of Jesus to the Christian faith? (Romans 1:4; 1 Corinthians 15:14).

2. In what sense do we participate in the resurrection before we die? (Romans 6:9-11; Ephesians 2:4-6; Colossians 3:1).

3. What impact did the resurrection have on John in Revelation 1:17-20?

6.

JESUS THE WAY

I am the way, and the truth, and the life

John 14:6

This is the sixth of the 'I am' sayings in John's Gospel. Of them all, perhaps this is the most well known, and one of the most profound. It brings us to the very heart and essence of the gospel, of John's purpose in writing and of Jesus' purpose in this world.

These words were spoken in the context of Jesus giving comfort to the disciples. This great chapter begins, 'Let not your hearts be troubled.' This is a phrase that will recur in the chapter, and it is a theme that runs through this section of John's Gospel. We often refer to chapters 14 – 16 of John as the 'farewell', or 'valedictory', discourse of Jesus; in the same way that the Sermon on the Mount, at the beginning of

Jesus' ministry, anticipated the great themes of his preaching, so this 'sermon in the upper room' comes at the close of his ministry and under the shadow of Calvary. It recapitulates much of what Jesus has already taught, but also anticipates the future, looking to the other side of the cross, the resurrection and the coming of the Holy Spirit.

Both in chapters 12 and 13, John has told us about the trouble of Jesus' soul and heart: 'Now is my soul troubled ... for this purpose I have come to this hour' (12:27); 'Jesus was troubled in his spirit...' (13:21). It was not possible for Jesus to go to the cross without experiencing the troubling of his soul. For this he came, and now the impending experience of betrayal and of the cross troubles his heart.

Yet it is in this context — when Jesus is conscious of his own soul being troubled — that he turns to the disciples and says, 'Let not *your* hearts be troubled.' The reason he brings such comfort to them is that he can look beyond the events that cause his own soul to be troubled: he is going to the Father, to the house of many rooms, and he is going to prepare a place for his people. They must look at the cross in the light of heaven, as Jesus himself does.

It is when Jesus says to them that they know the way to that place that Thomas objects. 'How can we know the way?' he asks. Jesus' answer is: 'I am the way, and the truth, and the life.'

These words show that Jesus is divine

We have already noted that the 'I am' sayings have some things in common, not least the phrase 'I am' itself. In John 8:58 Jesus describes himself as the 'I AM', with a designation that links back to the revelation of 'the LORD' in Exodus 3. Every time Jesus describes himself in this way, we hear the echoes of that disclosure, so that the phrases disclose and reveal the deity of Jesus — he is the God of the Old Testament. He is the way, the truth, the life — words that are full of the glory of Jesus, of the divine Jesus, the supernatural Jesus, the Jesus whom John declares to have been in the beginning.

These words show that Jesus is unique

These words are full of the uniqueness of Jesus too. He does not say, 'I am *a* way', or '*a* truth', or '*a* life'. He uses the definite article — 'I am *the* way, and *the* truth, and *the* life' — and he emphasizes the uniqueness and unprecedented and unparalleled nature of his work and ministry. He closes every other way; he is not one possible religious way among many possible religious ways. He does not say to us that we can take our pick of world religions, and choose him if we like. He says that if we do *not* choose him, we are not on the way to

God at all. The choice is not between the religion Jesus offers and the religion others offer; the choice is between having him as the way to God, or not coming to God at all.

He is not one possible truth among many possible religious truths in the world. In this postmodern world of ours, absolute truth is not a welcome concept. We are meant to give equal respect to every religious ideology; my 'truth' is considered no more valid than your 'truth', even if they are mutually contradictory. This world tries to hold every religious idea and opinion as being equally valid, but Jesus doesn't come and offer his truth as one kind of truth among many; he says, 'I am *the* truth'; this is stand-alone truth, absolutely unique.

John Stott puts it like this: 'We talk about Alexander the Great, and Charles the Great and Napoleon the Great. But we cannot talk about Jesus the Great; we have to talk about Jesus the *Only*.' This is the one who speaks to us here — Jesus the Only.

These words are unchangeably true

So these words are full of the deity of Jesus and the uniqueness of Jesus; they are also full of the unchange-ableness of Jesus, as all these sayings are. He does not say, 'I was the way,' or 'I will be the way,' but 'I *am* the way.' The truth is the truth *now*, not past and not future, but unchangeably present. He does not claim to have been the life, or to become the life, but to *be* the life.

Right at this present moment, immutably so, Jesus is the way, the truth and the life. For two thousand years those who have followed Jesus have staked their whole lives and deaths and future eternity on the fact that there is nothing that can change this from its present tense. He *is* the same, yesterday, today and for ever (Hebrews 13:8). The years have not modified his ability to speak in this way, and the generations have not altered his ability to be the way, the truth and the life.

These words reveal the irony of the crucifixion

Why these three words? Why does Jesus use this particular combination of words at this point? I think we could emphasize, first of all, how ironic they are. After all, this Jesus, who says, 'I am the truth', is about to be crucified on the basis of a miscarriage of justice. The religious leaders are going to hire false witnesses to lie his way to the cross. This one who is truth, and speaks the truth, and bears witness to the truth, is going to be taken by wicked hands and condemned by lying tongues and, in the greatest act of injustice and untruth that the world has ever known, he will be crucified.

But it has to be like this — for him to be the truth he has to be crucified. For him to be the way, he has to go his way, the way God ordained for him. God has given him a commandment. He cannot stay in the upper room — he has to leave it precisely so that the world may know that he loves the Father (14:31). There is a way he must follow, and if he is to be the way for his people he must go the way God directs him, all the way to Calvary. If he is to be the life for his people he must go all the way into death, and his body must lie lifeless behind the closed door of a borrowed grave. He must go the way of the cross in order to be the way; he must be sold by the lie into the hand of the ruler of the world in order to be the truth; he must taste death for every man to be the life for his people. Yet it is only through the cross that Jesus is the way, the truth and the life for us.

These words sum up the message of John's Gospel

We could also comment on the way John has prepared us for this statement right through his Gospel. For example, the three words, 'way', 'truth' and 'life', all appear in the opening chapter of John, in the great prelude to his Gospel. This is the very heart of the message of this Gospel. In John 1:23, John quotes from Isaiah 40, where the prophet had spoken about the forerunner of the Messiah preparing the *way* of the

Lord. We are also told in 1:14 that grace and *truth* came by Christ. We are told in 1:3 that in him was *life*, and his life was the light of men.

The way, the truth and the life — these are the themes of John's Gospel. Indeed, one could argue that the concept of 'life' dominates the first twelve chapters of John, and that the theme of 'truth' dominates the closing part of the Gospel. John tells us in chapter 20 that the reason he is writing is so that we shall believe that Jesus is the Son of God, and that by believing we shall have life in him. In other words, the purpose John has in writing is to show us that there is a way to God, to testify to the truth of Jesus as the way to God and to demonstrate that there is life through trusting in Jesus as the way to God.

So, on a purely literary level, we have been prepared for this. This is a summary statement of everything John says in the Gospel. Indeed, the first three encounters Jesus had with people in this account pointed in this direction. Jesus met Nathanael in chapter 1 — the Israelite in whom there was no guile. One day, Jesus told him, Nathanael would see angels ascending and descending on the Son of Man, a reference that goes back to Jacob's experience at Bethel in Genesis 28.

What is the significance of this? To put it simply, it is to show us the glory of Jesus as the Mediator. There is communion between heaven and earth through him — he, and only he, is the way by which angels can come from heaven to earth and from earth to heaven.

If there is to be any traffic at all between heaven and earth, and communion between God and man, it can only be through the Mediator, through Jesus the *way*.

Then there was the meeting with Nicodemus, that Professor of Theology from Israel. He knew so much, yet knew so little. He wanted to discuss the great topics: the miracles of Jesus, the source of his power, the unique method of his teaching. Jesus says to him, 'You must be born again.' What did Nicodemus need? Not an all-night discussion on miracles; it was simply the presentation of the truth he needed, and Jesus was the *truth* Nicodemus needed to hear and to know.

In John 4 Jesus met the woman of Samaria. She had come to a well to draw water, but Jesus uncovered her true, personal, spiritual thirst. Nothing in the world could satisfy it. Her lifestyle hadn't satisfied her — it had left her more empty and thirsty than she had ever been. 'Come to this well,' said Jesus, 'and drink, and you will thirst again.' That was true literally, but it was also true morally — she had tasted the water from all kinds of wells, and tried to find happiness in many kinds of relationships, but her soul was empty and dissatisfied. Jesus offered a well of water springing up to everlasting life. Jesus was the *life* she needed.

So in these encounters — Jesus and Nathanael, Jesus and Nicodemus, Jesus and the woman — John has been preparing us for this. Jesus is the way — that is what Nathanael discovered; he is the truth — that is what Nicodemus discovered; and he is the life — that is what the Samaritan woman discovered.

> *These words reveal Jesus as Prophet, Priest and King*

I think there is also a reference here to the offices of Jesus. It's not explicit in John's Gospel, but running through the teaching of the Bible is the answer to the question: 'What is Jesus for us?'

He is our *Priest*. What is the function of the priest? It is to make a way into the presence of God. One of the Latin words for priest is *'pontifex'*, literally a bridge-builder. The priest opened a way of communion; his office was one of bridge-building. Here is our Priest — he is our way.

He is our *Prophet*. The people said as much earlier in his ministry, after Jesus had fed five thousand people: 'This is ... the Prophet' (John 6:14). What does the prophet do? He brings the truth from God. He tells us what we could otherwise never know. As our Prophet, the last, great, eschatological prophet — the one who fulfils the prophecy of Moses in Deuteronomy 18 that a prophet like Moses would ultimately appear — Jesus tells us truth that we could otherwise never have known. He tells us about himself. He is the truth. He reveals to us the will of God for our salvation. We could never know that apart from him.

He is our *King* — and as our King he conquers death. That is part of what John wants to emphasize in this Gospel: he leads us to the cross, but then to the empty grave — this Jesus has victory over death and over the grave. He rises with the power of an endless life, king of his people. He is the way, because he is the Priest. He is the truth, because he is the Prophet. And he is the life, because he is the King who has conquered.

So these words, which draw together the strands of teaching that have been dominant in Jesus' ministry and example, bring us to the heart of the gospel message. Jesus has made the way because he *is* the way; he reveals the truth because he *is* the truth; and he triumphs because he *is* the life.

These words reveal Jesus as the Mediator of the covenant

But there is another way in which we could interpret this unique combination of words. Jesus is the Mediator, but he is Mediator of a *covenant*. The Lord's Supper, for example, is inaugurated by Jesus as the sign and seal of that covenant; he says that the cup is the cup of the new covenant in his blood. Behind the Supper lies the idea of the covenant of God's grace.

That theme runs through the Scriptures. Everyone who is saved is saved because they are bound to God in an everlasting covenant, of which Jesus is the Mediator. This was David's hope at the end of his life; he had much pain and regret as he reviewed the past, but he had one great hope: God had made an everlasting covenant with him that was ordered in all things and secure (2 Samuel 23:5). That was all his desire. It must be all our desire also. The Lord's Supper is for those who can say, 'He has made with me an everlasting covenant,' for those who know that there is nothing they can bring before God for their salvation — it is not their righteousness or good works that saves them, but only the blood of the everlasting covenant.

As Jesus unfolds the farewell discourse, I think he is bringing us into the heart of the covenant — he is dwelling on his position as Mediator of the covenant and the blessings he secures for his people as their Prophet, Priest and King. The prospect of heaven itself hinges on the covenant. That is why the discourse concludes with the Lord's prayer in which he said that he had finished the work that the Father gave him to do.

But what does this have to do with the great statement of our text, 'I am the way, and the truth, and the life'? Let's remind ourselves of what the prophet Jeremiah teaches us about the nature of God's covenant with us. Jeremiah was given a vision of good figs and bad figs (chapter 24), good fruit that could be eaten and bad fruit that could not. God applied that in a remarkable way, as he thought about his people in exile in Babylon. Like good figs, God said, he was going to gather his people, and bring them back to the land.

They would be planted there, and they would be safe — no more exile, no more Babylon, no more captivity. God was going to restore the fortunes of his people (Psalm 126:1). God was going to turn back their bondage. God turned the captivity of his people around. He showed his covenant faithfulness and mercy in three ways.

God brings his people back

First, he brought them back to their land (Jeremiah 24:6). He made a way for them. He was the way. The covenant restored them and brought them home. That is what God does for sinners in the gospel. It is what happened to the wasteful, prodigal son, who turned his back on home. What a relief that was to him at first — no more bondage, no more rules, no more praying, no more of the yoke and burden of home! He was his own man at last.

But he squandered everything. When he realized his folly, he came home, and there was a welcome which went far beyond anything he expected and anything he deserved. He found a way home. The restlessness, the wastefulness and the emptiness of these prodigal years were now met by the forgiveness and provision of home. That is what it is like for someone to be converted. To become a Christian is to have an entirely new beginning. If anyone is in Christ he is a new

creation (2 Corinthians 5:17), she is a new person —
everything is different; the world is different.

To be born again is just to come home. It is to
return to the God against whom we sinned. So when
he says, 'I am the way', Jesus is echoing the teaching of
the prophet — God will bring his people back. The
years that the locusts ate (Joel 2:25), and that sin ran
away with and that were lived without God, don't
matter any more. Now that you are home, God casts
the sins of his people into the sea. He covers all the
sins of his people with the perfect righteousness of
Christ. The father of the prodigal doesn't ask him to
account for the money he gave him, doesn't ask for
receipts or explanations — he just welcomes him back.
Jesus does the same. He is the way. This is the essence
of the covenant: we have come back to God.

God gives his people a heart to know him

But in the covenant God also said this: 'I will give them
a heart to know that I am the LORD' (Jeremiah 24:7).
Isn't that beautiful? Or, as Jeremiah 31 puts it, following the promise that God would bring them back and
make them walk in a good way in which they would
not fall, 'They shall all know me, from the least of them
to the greatest' (Jeremiah 31:34). Nicodemus had so
much knowledge in his head about theology and

religion and the Bible, but he did not know God, because the truth had not set him free.

Do we know God? Jesus' words in 17:3 tell us that eternal life means that we know God. It is not a quantity of life that matters; it is a *quality* of life, in which we know God intimately and personally. Jesus, who is the truth, comes to us and gives us knowledge of God.

To be saved means to know God. He has come with the power of his truth to give a new life and a new heart, which warms to Christ and which beats to the rhythm of the gospel, a heart that loves everything to do with Jesus Christ. The Jesus who is the truth is the Jesus who gives the knowledge of God that is eternal life. To be in the covenant is to know him, to be bound to him as the one who brings us back and the one who enables us to know him.

God himself is the life of his people

Finally, in the covenant God said this: 'I will plant them and not uproot them' (Jeremiah 24:6). This is a beautiful image that runs through the prophet Jeremiah. Hosea uses it too; when he talks about the blessings of the covenant he says, 'I will be like the dew to Israel ... from me your fruit comes' (Hosea 14:5,8).

Psalm 92 describes those who have been planted by God's grace in God's house as having supernatural life running through them. Others fade in old age, but

God's people still bear fruit. Paul says it this way — the outer nature is wasting away (2 Corinthians 4:16). We are getting old. We are fading away; every breath is taking us closer to the grave, back to the dust. But the inner nature, in the covenant of grace, where God himself is the life of his people, is being renewed. The soul of God's people is like a watered garden. The inward man or woman is being renewed.

God is the life of his people. Without him we are dead. Without him we cannot grow and develop in holiness, but in him there is life. In the embrace of the covenant God is my way — he brings me home. In the embrace of the covenant God is the truth — he enables me to know him. And within the embrace of the covenant God is the life — he plants me and waters me and gives me life that will not end.

So do we know him? Is he for us the way, the truth and the life? Is he the Mediator for me, securing for me the blessings of God's covenant and all my salvation?

WHO ARE YOU, JESUS?

'I am the way, the truth and the life. No one comes to the Father except through me.'

Questions for further study and reflection

1. How can we believe in an exclusive Jesus when there are so many religions in the world?

2. Look up the following references to truth in John's Gospel and consider their importance and significance: John 1:14; 8:32; 17:17.

3. Jesus asks his disciples to believe in him (John 14:1). What do the following verses teach us in connection with believing in the truth of Jesus: John 14:11,29; 16:29-33?

7.

JESUS THE VINE

I am the vine

John 15:5

We are coming to the end of our studies in the seven 'I am' sayings of John's Gospel. These words cast their own distinctive light on Jesus as our unique, unchangeable Saviour. He is the great I AM, the one who bears Jehovah's name.

John is very fond of the number seven; it is a number which occurs repeatedly in the book of Revelation. Indeed, the number seven is significant throughout Scripture. From the beginning of creation a pattern of seven was established in our routine. It is a number that symbolizes perfection. It is also the number of the 'I am' sayings, and this is the last of them — 'I am the vine.'

To capture the full significance of this, we need to remember what is happening here. Jesus has been in the upper room with his disciples, and he has been comforting them. At the end of chapter 14 it is obvious that Jesus is leaving the upper room. He calls them to leave. By the beginning of chapter 18, he has spoken to the disciples about the Father, and to the Father about the disciples; now he comes to the Garden of Gethsemane.

Commentators interpret the sequence of events differently, but it seems to me that at the end of chapter 14 Jesus and his disciples leave the upper room, and everything said in chapters 15 through 17 is spoken between the room and the garden, along the pathways of the Mount of Olives. There are vineyards all around; as one commentator puts it, 'Israel was a land of vineyards.' The vineyards and olive groves in this setting may have suggested this picture to Jesus, as he and the disciples walked towards Gethsemane (a name which itself, incidentally, means 'wine press'). The industry around the vineyards and olive groves of Israel, therefore, was much in Jesus' mind as he said, 'I am the true vine.'

But more than his physical surroundings was in his mind when he uttered these words, for there are many passages in the Bible which refer to vineyards. Psalm 80:8-11, for example, refers to Israel as a vine which was transplanted, taken out of Egypt and planted in another location. God's church, God's vineyard, took root in the land of Canaan and spread its branches all over the world. The prayer of Psalm 80 is that God would visit his own vine.

The prophets again and again take up the theme comparing God's people to a vineyard. But often this imagery is used by the prophets as they charge God's people with unfaithfulness and disobedience to the Lord. According to Isaiah 5:7, 'The vineyard of the LORD of hosts is the house of Israel,' yet the context of the passage is that the vineyard has not given the fruit for which it was designed; instead of giving grapes, it yielded wild grapes (v. 4). Instead of justice God found bloodshed, and an outcry instead of righteousness (v. 7). Similarly, in Ezekiel 15 the prophet declares that Jerusalem is a useless vine, fit only to be used for firewood. God is going to reject his people as worthless and valueless vines. They are fit for nothing.

Passages like Isaiah 5 and Ezekiel 15 feed into the seventh 'I am' saying; when Israel failed to serve God as they ought, Jesus comes and says, 'I am the true vine.' Here he may well be identifying himself as the true Israel, the true servant of Jehovah, the obedient servant who has come to give his life as a ransom for many. When Jesus describes himself in this way, it is in contrast with all that has gone before: God's people failed to honour and serve him; God needs to act decisively to provide a Saviour.

The Father tends the vines

Jesus is the true vine, and God the Father is compared to the person who dresses the vines, looking after them, pruning and caring for them so that they will bear good fruit. The Father tends to the vines. This is an important emphasis; everything that Jesus is doing he is doing in obedience to the Father. That emphasis runs throughout John's Gospel. The last thing he said in leaving the upper room was that he was going to show the world how much he loved, and loved to obey, his Father (14:31).

We must never lose sight of the fact that our salvation is the result of Jesus' relationship to his Father. God loved the world and gave his Son (3:16). The Son loved the Father and gave himself. Without the revelation of God as personal and triune, Father, Son and Holy Spirit, there is no gospel. Jesus loves the Father. He loves to obey the Father. He did not come to do his own will but the will of the Father (6:38). When we follow Jesus all the way to Calvary, we see him doing what the Father wishes him to do.

The Father is superintending all the events that lead up to the cross. Jesus is willingly going to the cross as the servant of Jehovah. So what does this Father do? He has come now to look after the vine, and to tend to the vineyard. Every branch that does not bear fruit he casts off, and every branch which does bear fruit he prunes in order to make it even more fruitful.

There has been a lot of needless discussion over these words. Does Jesus mean to teach by them that it is possible to be in him, and yet to be lost? The surface meaning of the words is that branches in Christ that are fruitless are cast away. It does seem to teach that it is possible to be in the vine, but to be lost through fruitlessness.

But of course that cannot be true; otherwise it would contradict other clear passages of Scripture which teach the eternal security of the believer. The point of the passage is not to teach temporary salvation. It is not possible to be saved today and lost tomorrow. To be in Christ at all is to be in Christ for ever. Salvation depends not on us, but on him. It depends on his grace. And once grace unites a sinner to the Saviour, there is nothing, nothing on earth, or in heaven or in hell, that can disunite or separate us from him.

The relationship between Jesus and his people is secure for ever. But Jesus is using the analogy of someone looking after the vine to illustrate one aspect of Christian living — the pruning work of God as a means of leading to further usefulness and fruitfulness. He wants to concentrate on the most important part of this — the fact that those who are in him are looked after and tended by the Father.

A stern warning

Having said that, I cannot read these words without thinking that perhaps on the mind of Jesus was the disciple who, to all intents and purposes, gave every impression that he was in Christ. There was a disciple of whom, if we were to see him, we would say, 'There is a good-living man, a good Christian, a good believer.' We would comment on the time he spent in Jesus' company and in the company of the other disciples. We might comment on the responsibilities he carried as a member of the band of disciples. We might comment on how busy he was — yet, for all these things, he was lost. Visibly he was in Jesus, but he was not actually in Jesus at all.

Judas Iscariot gave every impression that he was a true believer in Christ, but it was all apparent. To look at him you would have thought that this was a good man; if ever there was a believer, you would have said that this man was a believer. He was looking after the money, after the purse and every practical need of the disciples. Yet all of this belied the truth; John tells us that Judas went out into the night because Satan entered into him (John 13:27). Christ pronounced upon him the curse of the covenant: 'The Son of Man goes as it is written of him, but woe to that man by whom the Son of Man is betrayed! It would have been better for that man if he had not been born' (Matthew 26:24).

Judas stands before us as a stern warning. It is not possible for anyone to be *genuinely* converted and then actually lost, but it is possible for someone to be *apparently* converted and then actually lost. It is not enough that we give every outward indication that we are true believers. We may be strangers to God's grace, though apparently saved. We may be admitted visibly into the church, and be part of her life and structure and work in the world; to that extent we may be like branches in the vine. But if we are not spiritually united to Christ, our connection to his church will stand for nothing.

We do not assume that a person is a believer because of church blessings and privileges. The means of grace — Bible reading, gospel preaching, family prayers — are great privileges, but we cannot assume conversion or genuine Christianity because of them. God shows his goodness to us in these provisions, but his goodness will only condemn us if we do not come to repentance and faith in Jesus Christ. This is the solemn warning at the end of the Sermon on the Mount, as Jesus anticipates many coming to him at last with the argument: 'Lord, Lord, did we not prophesy in your name, and cast out demons in your name, and do many mighty works in your name?' Jesus does not say he will contradict their claim, but he does say that he will say to these people, 'I never knew you; depart from me, you workers of lawlessness' (Matthew 7:22,23). That is the truth set before us here — the frightening possibility that our lives too may be a combination of mighty works and lawlessness.

What a terrible thing for Judas to have had such exposure to Jesus, such time with him and such knowledge of his teaching, and then to be lost! How can we read the passage about fruitless branches of the vine being cast away without thinking of Judas Iscariot going out into the night to do Satan's work?

So when Jesus says that he is the vine and his people are the branches, what is he teaching us? Perhaps we could answer that question by asking other questions.

What is the purpose of the gospel?

What is the thing that makes the good news good? What is God looking for when he gives us the Bible and tells us about the way of salvation? What is behind it all? What is the end result of everything that the Bible teaches?

The answer to that question is in this passage: the ultimate aim to which all of this is pointing is that we should glorify God. That is why the first question of the *Shorter Catechism* is what it is. Man's chief purpose, and the main aim and end of his life, is to glorify God and to enjoy him for ever. That is what the gospel is about. God deserves to be glorified, and ought to be glorified by us. The tragedy of our sin is that we fail to glorify him as we ought.

Paul puts it like this in Romans 1: instead of glorifying God as they should, men turn away from God to worship the creature and the creation rather than the Creator. That is where our world is, and where our generation is. We are living in a world of man-worship; yet the whole end and purpose of our lives is that we should glorify God. 'By this is my Father glorified...', he says in this passage.

That is what Jesus is doing with his life — he is giving glory to the Father in obedience and service to him. Why is Jesus coming all the way to the cross? Why is he laying down his life for people like us? He is doing it to glorify his Father, so that God will be honoured and magnified in his life. If we are to be like Jesus, that must be the aim of our lives. By nature we turn away from God to man, away from the Creator to the creature — we come short of the glory of God (Romans 3:23).

God gave his Son for us in order that we might glorify the Father through him. The blood was shed at Calvary precisely so that we might glorify the Father; in our life and in our death we are asked to give all the glory to God. Is this happening in our lives? Have we come to recognize that this is the end of the gospel — that we should give glory to the Father?

How are we to glorify the Father?

What will glorify the Father? Jesus tells us in John 15:8 that what gives glory to the Father is that we bear much fruit. If we are to realize our chief purpose, and give glory to God in our lives, it can only be as these lives become a garden where choice fruits grow, a place where there will be fruit to glorify him.

Jesus draws on the illustrations of the vineyards — the olives, the grapes, the fruit-bearing trees with which Israel was familiar — and he emphasizes the need for fruit-bearing. I need to be a fruit-bearer, and I cannot be a fruit-bearer unless I have the life of God in my soul. That is the whole point of the analogy: the branch is where the fruit is borne, because the life in the vine extends into the branches, and that life is seen in the fruit, and the fruit glorifies the Father.

Let me extend the analogy. What do you think when you see a well-kept garden? You stand admiring it, admiring the order, the loveliness, the planting scheme. What do you think? You praise the gardener! You realize that this does not happen by itself. Gardens don't grow themselves: someone has been busy. Leave the ground to itself, and it bears thorns and thistles and weeds, and it is an untidy mess. But work it, get the hand of a gardener involved in it, get someone to prepare the ground and sow the seed, planting, arranging, watering, pruning — then there will be something new, something glorious and beautiful.

Jesus uses the same analogy here. What is it that will enable others to say that God has been at work in my life? Will they praise the extraordinary if I just live the same way that the world lives, leading an empty, meaningless life that simply gets carried along by the stream? No, that kind of life is growing wild like a wilderness. But if my life is different it is because someone has been at work in it. A gardener has been at work.

Isaiah and Jeremiah describe God's people as being like 'well-watered gardens'. Take a holy life, a life lived for the glory of God, a life that goes against the stream, that is not taken up with the meaninglessness of a fallen world, one that has found something worth living and dying for, and you can say that the hand of the gardener has been at work in it. God is glorified because there is fruit there that does not appear where the ground has been left wild and uncultivated.

Our lives need to be cultivated by the gardener so that the work of his hand and the seeds of his planting will be evident. Bearing fruit for God — that is the test of our lives. Is there anything in our lives to show that there is something spiritual, other-worldly, Christ-centred and God-glorifying there? 'This,' says Jesus, 'will glorify my Father — that you bear much fruit and be my disciples.'

| How can we bear fruit? |

If I cannot do it by myself; if my life needs to be changed, what must happen? What do I need more than anything else? How am I going to bear fruit?

There is only one answer to that question — I need to be in Christ, as a branch in the vine. The branch cannot bear fruit by itself, unless it abides in the vine. I need to abide in Christ if I am to be a fruit-bearer. Apart from Christ I can do nothing.

This is where the analogy of the vine is taking us — to the most fundamental issue of all, at the very heart of the gospel. It is saying that we need to be united to Jesus Christ. It is saying that by ourselves we are helpless and hopeless and fruitless. No matter what effort we make, and what good things we are able to do ourselves, we can do nothing. Maybe the first step to real, genuine conversion has to be that sense of absolute and utter helplessness. If I am to glorify the Father, it must be by fruit-bearing, and if I am to bear fruit I need to be in him.

Jesus says, 'If I am in you, and you are in me, then you will bear fruit.' Only then can the life that is in Jesus flow into us, and we shall bear fruit. Jesus is talking about a relationship between himself and his people that parallels and is analogous to the relationship between himself and his Father. As the Father loves the Son and is in him, so he loves us and is in us.

Think of that — think of the life of the Father in the Son, and that of the Son in the Father, interpenetrating one another in perfect harmony, union and reciprocity; and now Jesus says that I must have the same kind of relationship with him as he has with the Father. The one is in the other; there is perfect fellowship and unity between Father and Son; and there must be the same union between us and Christ.

Psalm 128 describes the blessing of God evident in the fruitfulness of a marriage union. The wife is described in the psalm as a fruitful vine in consequence of her union with her husband. The union of marriage is a mystery — two become one. That is how it is, Paul says, between Jesus and his church — two become one (Ephesians 5:31-32).

Think of the branches of a tree. Where does the branch begin? It grows out of the trunk. It is possible to distinguish trunk from branch, yet impossible to say where the one stops and the other begins. They are one entity, fused together and naturally joined together so that the same life is in both.

That is how it is between a saved sinner and his Saviour. If God is to be glorified and we are to bear fruit, it is because of that union. Are we so united to Jesus that he fills our lives, and we are absorbed with him, and he becomes our very existence, so that we can say with Paul that 'for us to live is Christ'?

What is it all about? It is about the Father being glorified in our lives.

How is the Father glorified in our lives? If we bear fruit.

How do we bear fruit? By being in the vine.

Who is the vine? Jesus says, 'I am the vine.'

It all comes back to him, and it comes down to him. What do we think of Christ? What is our relationship to him? It is not a matter of church involvement, or Bible knowledge, or theological ability, but a living, personal relationship with Jesus. He has life in himself, and it is the glory of the gospel that the life that is in him can flow into us. If it does not, then we remain dead in our trespasses and sins. Like Jerusalem in Isaiah's allegory and in Ezekiel's preaching, like the branch that does not bear fruit, then we are fit for nothing but to be cast away.

It is wonderful to think of Jesus, to spend time studying these great 'I am' sayings, to see him and watch him among men. But we need to be in him. We come into the world without him, far away from him, separated from him by our sin. We need to be in him, as branches in the vine. We can only come to be in him by grace. Then the marriage union will be complete, and it will go on until the day that we are with him, as all his people will be.

'Tis a point I long to know,
Oft it causes anxious thought:
Do I love the Lord or no?
Am I his or am I not?

Are we in him, in the vine, fruit-bearing branches, glorifying the Father? Nothing else matters quite like this. In him there is everything — life in its fullness and the blessing of God Almighty. May we have grace to seek him while he may be found, and to call on him while he is near!

WHO ARE YOU, JESUS?

'I am the vine; you are the branches. Whoever abides in me and I in him, he it is that bears much fruit, for apart from me you can do nothing...
'By this my Father is glorified, that you bear much fruit and so prove to be my disciples.'

Questions for further study and reflection

1. What do the following verses teach us about the believer as a fruit-bearer: Isaiah 58:11; Hosea 14:8; Galatians 5:22-24?

2. How does Paul use the image of a tree and branches in Romans 11:17-24?

3. What is the reference to a Branch in Jeremiah 23:5-6?

4. In what ways does God prune us to make us fruitful? (John 15:2).

CONCLUSION

In these short studies we have reflected on seven powerful images that Jesus uses of himself in the Gospel of John. Together they paint a vivid picture for us of what Jesus does for sinners, as he feeds them, enlightens them, protects them, cares for them, guides them and guarantees both their spiritual fruitfulness and their eternal security.

These seven sayings are a reminder to us that, to paraphrase Martin Luther, our salvation is altogether outside of ourselves. Faith means looking away from ourselves to another, to the changeless, glorious Christ who is God manifest in the flesh.

May we all come to know him, love him and serve him all our days, and discover that, amid all the changes of our experience, he remains the unchangeable 'I AM'!

NOTES

Chapter 2 — Jesus the light
1. B. B. Warfield, *Selected Shorter Writings* (Phillipsburg, New Jersey: Presbyterian and Reformed, 2005), vol. II, p.689.
2. *Ibid.,* p. 692.

Chapter 3 — Jesus the door
1. D. Martyn Lloyd-Jones, *Studies in the Sermon on the Mount* (London: IVF, 1962), vol. 2, p.221.

Chapter 4 — Jesus the shepherd
1. *Grace Hymns,* no. 390.

When Christ said, 'Before Abraham was, I am,' he declared himself to be the transcendent, eternal Lord beyond all comprehension. But Jesus also taught us that he is near to us in seven more 'I am' statements: 'I am ...' the bread, the light, the door, the shepherd, the resurrection, the way, truth and life, and the vine. Iain Campbell's meditations help us to eat the bread, see the light, enter the door, follow the shepherd, experience the resurrection, travel the way and abide in the vine that Christ is. Take, read and discover that Christ really is all that you need.

Joel R. Beeke
President, Puritan Reformed Theological Seminary,
Grand Rapids, Michigan